A LONG LABOUR

On behalf of my Mother

Judy Shandler

The Netherlands

North Sea

● Leeuwarden

Amsterdam ●

● Apeldoorn

● Amersfoort

● Rotterdam

Maas River

Germany

Rhine River

Belgium

● Maastricht

A LONG LABOUR

A DUTCH MOTHER'S HOLOCAUST MEMOIR

RHODEA SHANDLER

INTRODUCTION BY
S. Lillian Kremer

AFTERWORD BY
Roxsane Tanner

RONSDALE PRESS &
VANCOUVER HOLOCAUST EDUCATION CENTRE

A LONG LABOUR
Copyright © 2007 Rhodea Shandler

RONSDALE PRESS
3350 West 21st Avenue
Vancouver, B.C., Canada V6S 1G7
www.ronsdalepress.com

Typesetting: Julie Cochrane, in New Baskerville 11 pt on 15
Cover Design: Denys Yuen
Cover Photo: Rhodea as a young woman; Arnhem's destroyed bridge
Back Cover Photo: Rhodea's two children born during the war — Elly
    and Johanna
Paper: Ancient Forest Friendly "Silva" — 100% post-consumer waste, totally
    chlorine-free and acid-free

Ronsdale Press wishes to thank the following for their support of its publishing program: the Canada Council for the Arts, the Government of Canada through the Book Publishing Industry Development Program (BPIDP), and the Province of British Columbia through the Book Publishing Tax Credit program and the British Columbia Arts Council.

Library and Archives Canada Cataloguing in Publication

Shandler, Rhodea, 1918–2006.
    A long labour: a Dutch mother's Holocaust memoir / Rhodea Shandler; introduction by S. Lillian Kremer; afterword by Roxsane Tanner.

ISBN 978-1-55380-045-3

    1. Shandler, Rhodea, 1918–2006. 2. Holocaust, Jewish
(1939–1945) — Personal narratives. — 3. Jews — Netherlands — Biography.
4. Dutch Canadians — Biography. I. Title.

DJ283.S43A3 2007   940.53'18092   C2007-901793-2

At Ronsdale Press we are committed to protecting the environment. To this end we are working with Markets Initiative (www.oldgrowthfree.com) and printers to phase out our use of paper produced from ancient forests. This book is one step towards that goal.

Printed in Canada by Marquis Book Printing, Montreal

*To my parents,
brother, family and all
Holocaust victims*

ACKNOWLEDGEMENTS

I would like to thank my daughter Judy Shandler for her help with the manuscript. When I began writing this memoir she was invaluable in reading and editing what I wrote. She helped also in asking me questions so as to enable me to go back into my past and bring it to life again. I would also like to thank the Vancouver Holocaust Education Centre for arranging for Bettina Stumm to come to my home with her tape recorder to ask further questions so as to fill in the missing parts of the memoir. Bettina faithfully transcribed my accounts and became a friend to me in the process. When she encountered any confusion between my accounts, she would carefully clarify the material so that the memoir would be as accurate as possible. Without my daughter Judy and Bettina, this memoir would never have been brought to a conclusion. I cannot thank them enough. Needless to say, however, I take full responsibility for any errors of fact or omission in the memoir. I have tried my best to speak truthfully of what I know and experienced.

Special recognition is extended to Morris Wosk, z"l, businessman, community leader and philanthropist and to his son Rabbi Yosef Wosk, who, though a major gift to the Vancouver Holocaust Education Centre in 2000, established the Wosk Publishing Program. In recognition of the Wosk family's deep interest in Jewish history, the mandate of the Wosk Publishing Program is to publish original writings that advance our understanding of the events of the Holocaust, its history, implications and effects.

Thanks are also extended to Dr. Lillian Kremer for her Introduction and to Roxsane Tanner, who, speaking for her brother and sisters, contributed the Afterword.

CONTENTS

Introduction

S. LILLIAN KREMER

Rhodea Shandler's *A Long Labour: A Dutch Mother's Holocaust Memoir* is best understood within the context of the larger Dutch Jewish Holocaust experience and women's Holocaust narrative. The Dutch suffered enormous hardship during five years of occupation by Nazi Germany. Beginning in 1940, Dutch Jews were systematically identified and isolated. From 1942 to 1944 virtually all the nation's Jews who neither fled Holland nor were in hiding were deported to Bergen-Belsen, Theresienstadt, and the killing camps, primarily to Auschwitz-Birkenau and Sobibor from Westerbork and Vught Dutch transit camps. The fortunate few in hiding who avoided death among the ranks of underground resistance fighters or during the Dutch-wide "hungerwinter" of 1944–1945 experienced constant fear of detection and denunciation, physical deprivation and psychological anxiety throughout the occupation.

Whereas two of every three European Jews were murdered in the *Shoah*, three of every four Dutch Jews perished. Dutch civil servants cooperated in the disenfranchisement of Jewish citizens, stamping J's on their identity documents, confiscating their bicycles and radios, and sending unemployed Jews to labour camps. Dutch police actively participated in the deportations, and collaborators routinely facilitated Nazi objectives.

Following liberation, the surviving Jewish remnant found that their gentile compatriots were, in the main, disinterested in their experience and focused instead on their own hardships under Nazi occupation. In the late 1960s, Holland encountered the generation gap that affected other European nations. The older generation was de-mythologized, students criticized the "establishment," unmasked the resistance myth, exposed the lie of a widespread heroic response to Nazism by their parents, and began to pay more attention to the Dutch Holocaust experience. With publications such as Jack Presser's *Ondergang* (*Ashes in the Wind*) mapping the abandonment and betrayal of Dutch Jewry despite its integration in Dutch society, the nation began to confront the past more objectively. Historians Dick van Galen Last and Rolf Wolfswinkel (*Anne Frank and After: Dutch Holocaust Literature in Historical Perspective*), who chart the changing tides of interest from focus on the collective history to focus on individual stories, observe that since the 1970s, World War II literature and film have been welcomed in Holland, with resistance and collaboration the most popular subjects in general literature and the Holocaust a major theme for Jewish writers.

Dutch Holocaust literature documents conditions of Jews in hiding and incarcerated in the transit camps awaiting deportation to the killing centers, records the paradoxical role of the Jewish Council, and the survival struggle within the concentration camp universe. Among the victims writing of their ordeals while they were occurring are Anne Frank, who recorded her experience of being in hiding with her family, and Etty Hillesum and Philip Mechanicus, who described the horrendous physical conditions and camp administration of Westerbork and the psychological terror of inmates awaiting deportation. Other writers offered testimony at war's end. Upon his return from Bergen-Belsen, Abel Herzberg analyzed the behaviour of inmates and their reaction to the harsh camp conditions. Many years following liberation, Gerhard Durlacher recorded his experiences in occupied Holland, Theresienstadt and Auschwitz. Marga Minco addressed her wartime experience through the perspective of a fifteen-year-old narrator charting the incremental development of isolation and oppression in a narrative style blending directness and constraint.

Others wrote not only of the occupation and of the camp universe, but focused on the plight of survivors living in silence, shame, and anger as they recognized the magnitude of Dutch Jewish losses and Dutch collaboration. The war and the Holocaust, as well as its aftereffects on his generation, are consistent threads in the fiction of Harry Mulisch, one of the most important writers of the postwar generation. Judith Herzberg, the daughter of Holocaust chronicler Abel Herzberg, who had initially intended to leave the subject to her father, writes about the continuing impact of the Holocaust past on the present, emergence of wartime trauma among characters who have refrained from breaking silence, the tensions within a survivor family and those between Jews and Dutch non-Jews. Her autobiographical writing illuminates the pain of a child hidden apart from her parents, the experience of living under a false identity and being reunited with her parents. From the vantage point of an adult returned to Judaism, Andreas Burnier, who survived the war hidden separately from her parents, writes of a family reunion marred by the hidden child's Holocaust-wrought contempt for Judaism born of her internalization of her protector's anti-Semitism. She recounts recurrent traumatic experiences of displacement and betrayal, of the emotionally wrenching need to remain silent while listening to the anti-Semitic ranting of rescuers, and of the Dutch, who contrary to the myth of rescue, were indifferent to the fate of the Jews or betrayed them when that proved to be opportune.

In the 1980s, a new paradigm of second-generation writing explored issues of memory and Holocaust impact on the lives of children of victims, bystanders, and perpetrators. Arnon Grunberg's autobiographical fiction delineates the stress for children growing up with adults suffering from survivor syndrome. Similarly, Carl Friedman renders pressures created by Holocaust-wounded parenting: one parent who constantly talks of *Shoah* pain and is emotionally needy, the other who maintains a code of silence and emotional distance. Rather than receding into the past, the impact of the Holocaust continues to impinge on the present as the postwar generation grapples with parents' histories and the psychological imprint it has encoded their lives.

Rhodea Shandler, who survived the Holocaust hiding in rural Holland, lived in Canada from 1951 until her death in 2006. Having immigrated to Canada because she despaired of the diminishment of Dutch Jewry and Dutch disinterest in Holocaust history, she waited many decades before committing her memories and reflections to print. The long delay might be explained by the demands of raising eight children, the anguish of dredging up painful memories, and the formidable challenge of finding the right words to tell her story. Motivated, in old age, by a desire to leave her story for her children, she remembers and movingly commemorates her murdered family members, reveals her Holocaust history, and meditates on its postwar impact.

In *A Long Labour: A Dutch Mother's Holocaust Memoir*, Shandler delineates her direct experience of many aspects of Dutch Jewry's encounter with Nazi occupation in a manner that echoes the conventions and themes of women's Holocaust writing. Her title invokes pregnancy, common in women's Holocaust experience and writing, thereby testifying to the female particularities of her Shoah memories and the long gestation process from recollection to representation. Holocaust commemoration appears as literary theme and in the narrative form; thematically through the survivor's need to communicate history and foil its misappropriation; and, in narrative structure, as memoir. In contrast to the conjoining of an unmediated direct connection with the recorded events and the expressive point of view of the diarist, Shandler's distanced retrospective stance combines reportage with mediated recollection, information gleaned from other survivors and postwar documentation. Unlike the diarist's vision limited to the writer's wartime knowledge that may have been clouded by Nazi deception or by insufficient access to information, the survivor's postwar perspective permits the conjunction of the immediacy of the victim's perspective as well as a postwar assessment of traumatic *Shoah* experience, and of the impact of the past on the present.

Shandler synthesizes three characteristically separate roles: the victim who experiences, the eyewitness who reports, and the imaginative narrator who reconstructs or transfigures historic events. When she writes of the trauma of hiding and frequent relocation to avoid capture she does so as an eyewitness, from inside the Nazi universe. When she writes of her brother's work and death at Auschwitz, she does so as indirect witness reporting a family friend's direct witness, carefully delineating and differentiating perception and narrative voice while anchoring and validating the writing in reality. When she writes of Allied movements, or the progress of the war, she does so having been informed by her husband who received information from resistance contacts or access to British radio broadcasts, and when she writes of the different categories of Westerbork prisoners, she writes as a researcher of that Holocaust history.

As in the works of other survivor writers, the reader senses two distinctive voices in Shandler's memoir — the harried voice of the immediate experience and the reflective voice, the youthful Holocaust era point of view and the more comprehensive and meditative post*Shoah* authorial intelligence. We recognize distinctions between the "I" of the narrative present, in accounts rendered from within the perspective of the Nazi designed universe and the "I" of the mature writer perceiving the events of the narrative through a postHolocaust lens.

Shandler presents a detailed account of her family's metamorphosis from Dutch citizens to fugitives and victims of the Third Reich within the larger context of Dutch Holocaust history.

Having come from a family that considered itself "so integrated into the general Dutch community that on many occasions we didn't think ourselves so very different from the Dutch — that is until the Nazis announced otherwise," Shandler charts the life her family enjoyed prior to the Nazi occupation: good employment, good relations with the larger community only occasionally marred by antisemitic slurs, and freedom to live openly as observant Jews who kept the Sabbath and dietary laws, celebrated holidays, and attended synagogue regularly. Like many Dutch Jews, her family members suffered loss of income requiring support by the Jewish National Fund.

Contextualizing the family experience within the larger realm of Dutch Jewish experience, Shandler provides political insight noting that since Holland was a democracy, it tolerated the presence of an anti-Jewish political party, the National Socialist Movement that shared German Nazi ideology. With the growth of influence of this party, Jews began to encounter economic hardship and social ostracism. Once Holland succumbed to Nazi rule, the lives of Dutch Jews changed radically under anti-Jewish legislation, including dismissal from civil service positions, curtailment of Jewish professional activities, closure of universities with large Jewish enrollments, banning from residential options in the Hague and other coastal areas, exclusion from coffee shops and restaurants, mandatory registration, the humiliation of wearing a yellow star, and carrying an official identity card branded with a "J." Anti-Jewish legislation led in 1942 to the deportation of the Jews, including the author's parents, her brother and his family to Westerbork and from there to Auschwitz, never to return.

Shandler carefully charts her experience from prewar normality to separation from family and fugitive status hiding among gentile families in remote rural areas of northern Holland. As a young adult in 1940, Shandler trained to be a nurse and worked in a private Jewish hospital. During this time, she conceived a child out of wedlock with a German Jewish refugee eleven years her senior who, as a Gestapo fugitive, could not legally marry. Gestapo arrest and deportation of the infant's father and Shandler's untenable social position led her to send the infant to live with her married sister. On the eve of marriage, two years later, to Ernst Bollegraaf, a Dutch Jew, the couple's happiness was shattered when they learned that their parents along with Shandler's brother and his family had been incarcerated in Westerbork. Typical of the couple's coping strategy is Shandler's subsequent description of the efforts she and her husband made to live normal lives: "to find stability beyond the tragedies of the present and insecurity of the future by functioning in patterns that we recognized as stable and secure in the past" (58).

Representative of the memoir's fusion of public and private Dutch Holocaust experience, recounting events directly witnessed by the narrator with those reported by other eyewitnesses or gleaned from postwar historiography or speculation is the author's distinctive narration of the Amsterdam and Rotterdam bombings that achieved Nazi victory over Holland in four days and instituted a hellish five-year occupation. Shandler and her medical colleagues were disabused of their assumption that a laboratory mishap had caused a sudden explosion at their hospital. They soon understood that they were witnesses to the initial 1940 air assault on Amsterdam. From their hospital vantage point, they discovered bombing and shooting all around them. The hundreds of objects they observed falling from the sky were parachutes carrying soldiers and equipment. The next morning the German tanks rolled into Amsterdam and the Dutch were virtual prisoners. Departing from the dramatic rendition of the Amsterdam bombing and distress at seeing swastika bearing flags and banners adorning official buildings and residences the following day, Shandler offers a summary second-hand report of German ships bombing Rotterdam harbor, and Holland's swift capitulation from the point of view of her brother-in-law who had been trapped in the rubble for several days.

A more developed instance of Shandler's fusion of communal and individual Holocaust history is her account of the Nazi clearing of the Jewish mental hospital in which she worked. Here, she vividly conveys the Nazi pattern of using victims to facilitate their crimes and strategic deceit in her description of coerced young Jewish Westerbork prisoners assisting in the transport of the patients on pain of their own incarcerated families being killed and Germans promising the medical staff and patients transport to a better facility. Her husband, who had been serving on the Jewish board of directors at Amersfoort, informed her in January 1943, of the imminent Nazi action at the hospital and urged her to leave. Aware that Nazis were systematically killing German mental patients, the Dutch medical staff released able and willing patients, providing them with food, train fare, and lodging expenses in anticipation of the German arrival. After several hours helping prepare and provision the patients, Shandler determined to save her own life and flee as her husband had urged.

Shandler's fraught description echoes Holocaust writing by those in similar angst and peril escaping a Nazi action: she leaves her possessions, removes her yellow star, and destroys her identification card. With scrupulous honesty, she conveys her anguished moral conflict as she urged fellow medical staff to join her in flight, offering them safety in her husband's large house, only to be perceived by her colleagues as traitorous. At the railroad terminus, her agony deepens as she distances herself from patients seeking her assistance and company, ignoring or denying their pleas, "unwilling and afraid to acknowledge them" (65). Characteristically, Shandler shifts from her dramatic eyewitness account to explain that she later learned many of the patients "had been picked up by the police and soldiers because of their frightened behaviour and outbursts" (66). Although Shandler does not identify the source of her knowledge in this instance, she describes the evacuation scene following her escape, the brutal loading of patients onto trucks and the train where they and unsuspecting medical staff were "pushed and bludgeoned to move faster, wedged body-beside-body into those windowless wagons. . . . No air could circulate, and the patients went mad: people could hear them screaming, having seizures, wildly hitting the walls and attacking each other in a total frenzy" (67). Representative of her effort to engage the situation she did not witness is her speculation of the deportees' behaviour on the train and their fate: whether only the patients or the entire trainload of passengers were gassed just across the German border, or whether the medical staff were sent to Auschwitz, or whether the entire group was brought first to Westerbork and then deported to Auschwitz (67–68). The tone of this passage is marked not only by the intensity of the fugitive's fear of capture as she posed as a confident traveller and casual shopper, but her moral agony, her shame as she left her patients, wondering then and long after whether she was a deserter.

At the heart of the memoir, in chapters titled "Hiding" and "Buried and Concealed," the author quickly makes the transition from anxiety-driven questions about discovery of her escape to the fundamentals of hiding and surviving among a population that while largely rejecting Nazi anti-Jewish ideology was not particularly pro-Jewish and needed to remain on good terms with the oppressive new rulers. This portion of the memoir has much in common with other Holocaust accounts of fugitives in hiding. She and her husband had "fake identity papers from Dutch citizens who had died" (88). Although she no longer remembers the surname, she answered to the name of Nelly and her papers indicated that she hailed from Delft. Moves were frequent, subject to the will of hosts who were themselves threatened by the presence of, or resentful of, their temporary guests. Persistent hunger, cold, and lack of adequate hygiene were commonplace. Physical discomfort was heightened by the threat of Nazi searches of the hitherto safe sanctuary necessitating concealment either within a small space behind an interior double wall with just enough space to stand or dangerous departure to hide in a nearby shed, ditch, or open field. In a particularly frightening scene, Shandler recounts hiding in a wooded area in a hole "less than a meter deep and just wide enough to lie down without moving around" (104). After she settled in with a blanket to keep dry, the farmer covered the hole with a board and camouflaged it with leaves and other ground cover. There she stayed in the company of insects and worms until the farmer deemed it safe to emerge.

The hiding experiences Shandler and her husband encountered ranged from genial to begrudging accommodation. Among the Dutch rescuers and betrayers who played roles in the Shandlers' fate was a couple who promised shelter in exchange for payment and delivery of provisions ample for an extended period only to take possession of their property and dispossess the victims a day later. Others agreed to safeguard property until the rightful Jewish owners could reclaim it after the war only to steal it; and other rare humanitarians welcomed the penniless and hounded Jews onto their farms and into their homes free of charge. Shandler also comments on the good will of neighbours who not only keep the secret of the farmers and their guests, but alert them to imminent Nazi searches. In most instances, the fugitive wife assisted the host family with housework, and her husband, who did not look Jewish, helped with outdoor farm work. In several locations, he played an active role in Underground operations including delivery of food stamps and messages to other fugitives, collecting coal and peat dropped by Dutch trainmen for distribution among local farmers, and joining in a resistance mission to feed trapped Allied military personnel.

Beyond incisive delineation of the physicality of being in hiding, Shandler clearly and movingly articulates the psychological angst that complicated physical survival, particularly concern about the fate of family members imprisoned in Westerbork. When she learned that her sisters had gone into hiding, Shandler grew concerned for the safety of her three-year-old daughter who had been in her sister's care but was then transferred to the protection of others. Even as she is tormented with guilt for failing to convince her parents to go into hiding, thoughts of a postwar family reunion sustain her throughout her fugitive years.

Holocaust narratives by women writers significantly extend literary representation and interpretation of the *Shoah* by introducing female-centered stories and underscoring the gender-specificity of the experience and coping patterns. Among the topics absent in male Holocaust writing — often presented and perceived as normative — are the ways motherhood further burdened women's Holocaust ordeals. Pregnancy and motherhood, prevalent in women's Holocaust writing as signs of female vulnerability or as reminders of the dominance of the life force, are mainstays of women's Holocaust writing. Nazi sexist and racist policies unavoidably cast mothers of "inferior races" as threats to Aryan purity and therefore destined them and their offspring for extermination. Jewish women discovered that bearing children was a crime against the Reich. Their children were denied life; condemned to starvation, disease, medical experimentation; doomed to be gassed or tossed alive into crematoria ovens and lime pits.

While Shandler did not endure the horrors the ghetto and camp mothers endured, she experienced the trepidation of a pregnancy as a fugitive, failing at an early attempt to abort the pregnancy, sustaining the fetus under onerous circumstances and suffering a painful clandestine delivery. She delineates not only the animus of hitherto generous hosts in whose barn she was living, but also the physical deprivations of inadequate food, lack of sanitation in the converted pigsty, and limited exercise adding to her physical discomfort. Signs of the hosts' displeasure with the Jewish couple included terminating the practice of allowing them to eat inside the family home, reduction of food so that the couple was now always hungry, and confinement to the converted pigsty. Like many pregnant Jewish women under Nazi domination, Shandler was overwhelmed by anxiety regarding the child's potential care and survival in Nazi Europe, how to feed her, keep her warm in winter, what to do if a passerby heard her crying. Shandler survived a painful December delivery in a frigid barn with only primitive, unsterilized equipment, aided by her husband and a fellow fugitive who had been a nurse before she went into hiding. The newborn's breathing was laboured and her skin "an unhealthy shade of blue" (93).

Despite the infant's silence during the first two months of her life, fear that she would eventually cry and the continued hostile response of their hosts prompted the next Resistance-assisted move for the family. Although Shandler laments the loss of their hosts' welcome, she acknowledges their legitimate fear of the presence of a wailing infant. The peril of the fugitives and the host families led the Resistance to secure separate hiding places for each of the three, the location of each to remain unbeknownst to the husband and wife. Shandler's living conditions improved considerably in her new location. She had a room inside the family home, once again worked as a housekeeper, cooking, sewing, cleaning, and doing laundry. In an ironic turn of events, she also served as a nanny for the hosts' children, a role that heightened her own maternal pain as she constantly worried about the welfare of her own children, "Where were they right now? What were they doing? How were they growing up?" (102)

Families who had the opportunity to hide usually separated to reduce the risk of losing everyone, or because it was more feasible to hide children than adults. The dilemma of whether to send children to safety among strangers or to remain together as a family was among the most emotionally wrenching in Holocaust experience and is a prevalent theme in much Holocaust narrative. When the decision was taken to place a child with Gentiles, the hidden were living outside the law, moving from place to place, obtaining false papers, "passing" as Christians, learning new names and new family histories. There was constant danger of neighbours suspecting that a Jewish child was being sheltered, or of the child's inadvertent self-betrayal. Children in "open" hiding who were passing as Christians lived in fear of blurting out their real names, of uttering a Jewish word, of mispronouncing a Christian prayer or forgetting an anticipated religious gesture. Heightening the psychological stress of undeviating vigilance was the pain of feeling abandoned by their parents.

The theme of parent/child separation and reunion, prominent in women's Holocaust writing, is also part of Shandler's experience. Children too young to understand either their religious identity or to have bonded closely with their parents and consequently untroubled by that dimension of an alien environment, as was the case with Shandler's daughters, often encountered psychological strain when forced to part from their rescuers to be reunited with their biological parents. Shandler, who reports only that which she witnessed or learned from others at a later date, is mum on the issue of the hidden child's religious perceptions for it did not affect sixteen-month-old Johanna directly and apparently may not have been an issue for her older daughter, given Elly's years in hiding from age three to five and her acceptance into her host family. However, removing them from homes where they had known safety and affection to live with virtual strangers was another matter.

Following liberation, Shandler and her husband expressed gratitude to those who saved their daughters but did not remove them from their caretakers' homes immediately. The Shandlers remained at the farm where they were hiding to help their benefactors with the harvest and to allow their toddler to be weaned from her family and grow accustomed to her parents. Similarly, Elly remained with her host family while she, too, adjusted to her biological parents and the rupture from those who cared for her after separation from her maternal aunt.

Shandler writes movingly, but unsentimentally, of the reunion with the reluctant older child she had not seen for two years, "She was suspicious and wary of us. 'I'm not going with you,' she informed me. 'Why not?' I asked. 'Because you won't bring me back,' she responded" (127). The mother, who claims not to have been heart-broken or very upset that Elly did not recognize her or want to depart from her place of refuge, confesses that she could hardly remember the child anymore either and recognized the need for transitional time with the protective hosts who risked their lives to save the child and truly loved her. Despite Shandler's gratitude for the strangers' care of her child, she is also dismayed as she recognizes that Elly's health was compromised because her hosts neglected some of her needs, having used a portion of the money the Underground provided for the child's care to feed their family. Much as the Shandlers wanted their children, they were sensitive both to the feelings of security the children enjoyed with their host families and the emotional disruption that reunion with their parents would engender and no less sensitive to emotional injury the separation would bring the hosts who had come to love the children.

Sustained during the war by ignorance of the true nature of the concentration camps and therefore hopeful of reunion with her deported family members, after liberation Shandler faced the cruel reality that they would never be seen again. Survivor guilt plagued her for the six decades she survived. She blamed herself for failing to convince the entire family to go into hiding. The lament for her parents' loss is a refrain throughout the memoir. She acknowledges early in the text that she and her husband felt they had let their parents down and that she is haunted by the recurrent question, "Why couldn't I save them?" (10). She confesses that despite the passage of sixty years, she cannot escape her memories or the plaguing question of why she and Ernst were spared and not her parents and nearly all of her family.

The Netherlands, like many nations of Jewish pre*Shoah* residence, neither recognized nor wanted to understand the enormity of the Judeocide and therefore largely ignored the survivors' unique history. All citizens were the same and were to be treated equally, and so the immensity of Jewish losses was disregarded and the survivors' sensibilities dismissed. Although Jewish legal rights were restored and anti-Semitism became less blatant, some Dutch perpetrators were prosecuted, and minimal compensation for lost property was provided, economic, social, and psychological assistance was minimal. That the Dutch non-Jews who had benefited from Jewish deportation were unwilling to return property or help Holocaust victims in any way is a source of the author's sadness and contempt. She recounts efforts she and her husband made to retrieve money and property left with friends, only to discover that those people had either made use of their goods during the war to assuage their own hardships or, simply pilfered them to enrich themselves. Theft and betrayal at almost every turn, postwar anti-Semitism, and grief for lost family and friends account for the Shandlers' decision to leave the place of their sorrows and pursue a new life of freedom in the land of the generous Canadian soldiers who helped liberate Holland. Despite finding freedom and a sense of peace in Canada, Shandler continued to suffer Holocaust memories and nightmares. Part of her, she insists "remains in hiding, silent, wandering" (159).

In a posthumously published diary, Etty Hillesum, a young Dutch Jewess who chronicled the atrocities perpetrated against Holland's Jews while she laboured in Westerbork transit camp before deportation to Auschwitz, wrote "I shall wield this slender fountain pen as if it were a hammer and my words will have to be so many hammer-strokes with which to beat out the story of our fate and of a piece of history as it is and never was before" (146). Similarly, Shandler — a young Dutch Jewish mother who escaped the horrors that Hillesum witnessed and experienced because compatriots sustained her — foils the erasure of history that revisionists seek. Rhodea Shandler narrates the history as it was for those fortunate few who survived through the mercy of fellow citizens who risked their own lives on behalf of their neighbors. Her memoir is rooted in psychological realism, anchored in historicity and the effects of the *Shoah* on the postwar lives of its victims.

* * *

S. Lillian Kremer, University Distinguished Professor Emerita, Department of English, Kansas State University, is the editor of *Holocaust Literature: An Encyclopedia of Writers and Their Work* and author of *Women's Holocaust Writing: Memory and Imagination* and *Witness Through the Imagination: Jewish American Holocaust Literature*.

BIBLIOGRAPHY

Hillesum, Etty. *An Interrupted Life: The Diaries of Etty Hillesum*, trans. Arnold J. Pomerans. New York: Pantheon Books, 1984.
van Galen Last, Dick and Rolf Wolfswinkel. *Anne Frank and After: Dutch Holocaust Literature in Historical Perspective*. Amsterdam University Press, 1996.

Rhodea as an infant with her father Joseph Dwinger and her mother
Kaatje Dwinger, 1918. Both her parents died in Auschwitz.
(Rhodea's original name was Henriette. After emigrating to Canada,
she changed her name to Rhodea).

The Cohen family, Leeuwarden, The Netherlands, 1914. Rhodea's grandfather, Benjamin Cohen, and his wife, Heintje Cohen-Cuovorden, are seated in the middle of the front row surrounded by their offspring with their spouses and their grandchildren. The photo was taken by Rhodea's father, Joseph Dwinger. Courtesy of Johanna Weijel-Dwinger and Elly Bollegraaf.

FRONT ROW (LEFT TO RIGHT): Kaatje Dwinger-Cohen, Johanna Dwinger, (Levi) Louis Cohen, Trui de Leeuw-Cohen, Cato de Leeuw, Benjamin Cohen, Heintje Cohen-Coevorden, Louis Cohen, Nathan (Jan) Cohen, Esther Cohen-Turksma, Abraham Cohen, Hartog Cohen, Benjamin (Bennie) Cohen.

SECOND ROW: Joseph Dwinger, Bertha Cohen-de Jong, Isaac de Leeuw, Judith Feitsma-Cohen, Philip Feitsma, Rachel Feitsma-Cohen, Benjamin (Beike) Feitsma, Kaatje Cohen-Feitsma.

BACK ROW (CHILDREN): Benjamin (Benno) Cohen, Meijer de Leeuw, Martha Feitsma, Simon Dwinger, Benjamin (Beike) Cohen, Zus (Heintje) Dwinger.

Rhodea's family. Left to right: Joseph Dwinger (father),
Heintje (sister), Simon (brother), Rhodea, Johanna (sister),
Kaatje (mother).

Rhodea as a child, modelling her native Friesland
costume for her father's photography studio.

Rhodea at age four.

Rhodea riding a donkey on a family holiday at
Scheveningen on the North Sea coast.

Rhodea's class photo for her "special Hebrew school" that she
attended on Sunday mornings and Wednesday afternoons
"for an hour or so." She is standing on the far right.

Rhodea's brother Simon. "He was very talented, a real prodigy."
He died in Auschwitz.

Rhodea at her violin lesson. "My abilities were only average."

Rhodea and her older sister Johanna outside their father's
photography studio in Leeuwarden, c. 1924.

CHAPTER 1

Fever

For the longest time I have been trying to write but it is not easy. I have learned that if I write things down they stop circling in my mind. Writing gives me release. But many times the words are not there. Just a fever. Other times I wake up, sit in the kitchen at five a.m., and start writing. Often, however, it sounds wrong and I have to tear it up and start over again. I find it hard to know where to begin. I have forgotten a lot about my life.

"Why am I writing this?" I ask myself. "Why is it so important to tell you about my life? Why, at this particular time, do I feel it necessary to do so? It is difficult to start writing about things that I have not talked about for so long. After the war nobody spoke about the Holocaust. My children didn't know anything about it since they were either born after the war or were too young to remember anything about it personally. And I never thought about writing at that time. There were too many other things to do. My husband and I had eight children to raise and ensure they received a good education. But the desire to write must have been there all along. Strange that the urge to write often comes after a time lapse. Perhaps there is sufficient distance now between the events and my recording of them for my mind to rest, to be able to make sense of those long-ago occurrences.

I also think it necessary to write about my life and experiences during the Holocaust because I am one of the few in my circle who actually feel compelled to do so. Why don't many more survivors want to write? Perhaps because they still think they are to blame for the Holocaust. I think we felt ashamed of what happened or were made to feel ashamed. Often survivors just want to block it out of their minds or keep it locked in their hearts where the anger still smoulders. It rips their souls apart because they cannot express the grief they carry. My sister Johanna, now in her nineties, cannot let go. She does not tell anyone what she experienced with her family. She is still angry and those thoughts continue to circle in her mind. She sits at home every day with no desire to meet people or find a friend with whom she could have some company or at least a conversation to get things off her chest. I tell her that if she can't write about it, perhaps she could at least talk about it on tape. But it is too difficult; she cannot bring herself to do it.

For much of the time, I try hard not to look back. If you look back and become trapped in the past, you are unable to go forward and might lose your way altogether. But at the same time I feel I must look back; my story must be told. Perhaps this *is* my destiny. What gives me an urge to write, while other people who have gone through the war and the Holocaust keep it inside themselves? I have to express my soul. Here I can fight injustice with words. The urge to write doesn't come from myself. I don't think we think with our brains. Our intelligence is like antennae picking up signals from a higher power. Maybe forces outside our existence tell me to write, to honour my parents by telling their story. I owe it to my father and mother and all the family who disappeared. I do not want them to have lived in vain. I also write for my children and future generations in order that they know what the Holocaust did to our family. I need to let go of what I witnessed. I hope that those who come after me can read it as history and learn to take the gift of human life seriously.

I am writing in the spring of 2005. This summer I am going to be eighty-seven, but I feel old and would like not to be reminded of my age. I'm not worried about living. I have my eight wonderful children, and in general I have been feeling happy lately. My happiness is often based on very simple things, like a couple of good writing pens. I finally bought some after a long time of buying and using those "Bic" throw-away pens. I also purchased some new cosmetics. Not that I am fashionable, but I had run out of them completely. An old lady needs to spruce herself up after she gets out of bed. My biggest improvement is my new Cadillac, my scooter. Now when the weather is good, I roll the scooter out without too much difficulty and away I go. I "drive" to the shopping centre or to the beautiful park behind the South Arm Community Centre. There are little hidden paths, a few bridges and beautiful green fields shaded by trees. It makes me think that even if the situations in the world do not look too bright, I am still very thankful. God has given me many blessings and much satisfaction. Deep down in my soul I know that the blessings in our family will be bountiful. The best is still to come, so I throw my blues away. Like a little child, my eyes are wide open and full of longing for the gifts still in store for us.

As I become older I worry less about dying. My husband died in 1987, so I do not have him with me anymore. My parents are not here. When death comes, it comes. I'm not looking for it, yet I am also not afraid of it. I'm satisfied with my life. I raised my children to be good people. My husband loved me. I am not plagued with regrets or self-doubts about my path in life. And I'm a strong believer in life after death. I feel much more pulled to the other side. Sometimes I think I'm sitting with my feet over there already.

In the mornings, awake and ready to enter the day, I sit on the edge of my bed for a long time, thinking, What am I going to do with myself all day? As I get older everything slows down. Except my brain. Sometimes I think that for those who lose their mental capabilities, growing older is easier. Finally, when I get going I often don't know where to go or what to do. Maybe because I have few people left and no one to fall back on, except my children. How I long to be able to go back to my home, not the home in which I live now but my parents' home, to get my love charged up. Maybe that is why we seniors love each other, because we no longer have our parents. My children love me and I'm quite sure that if I couldn't help myself they would help me. I really enjoy their company; we're always laughing together! I see my children as the future.

But there are virtually no people left from the past. There is Johanna, my sister who still lives in Holland, but no Jewish friends, aunts, or uncles that I knew before the Second World War. Most of them were taken away during the Hitler regime, punished for a non-existent crime, tortured, starved, abused and murdered. Impossible? It is possible. We did not know. We did not know where the transport trains were taking them. Sometimes, a letter arrived from a deported person to one of their family, letting them know they were working in a factory and that they were all right. Was it fake? Did some Nazi write this letter to make people believe this? Was the writer of this letter already turned into ashes?

This morning I think about my oldest sibling and only brother Simon and my parents. Both of my older sisters, Johanna and Henny, and their families survived the Hitler regime by going into hiding. But Simon and his family were taken away at the end of 1942. I heard that he worked for two years in the Auschwitz concentration camp where he must have known that his wife and children were dead. He must have seen the smoking chimneys in the distance. He was a strong young man of thirty-five and was chosen to work. The saying over the entrance of Auschwitz reads, "*Arbeit*

Macht Frei," but the sign was cruelly misleading; this "free" was all so temporary. How long is a man able to work when he has nothing to eat except watery soup and a hunk of bread? I feel how much my brother suffered. I feel his spirit and soul in me working. "Tell this to the world," he says, pointing to me.

My parents, Kaatje and Joseph, were also deported. They were in their early sixties at the time and would have been considered "old" by Nazi concentration camp standards. They would not have survived the selection. Initially, my parents were ordered to go to Westerbork, the holding camp in Holland, where they stayed for about two or three weeks. While they were there I was still able to communicate with them. My father wrote that they had met some friends in Westerbork and that the food wasn't bad. We sent them a few small food parcels, usually filled with bread, candies, and other treats until one came back unopened with the notice that they were already at their destination — Poland. After that we heard nothing. How would they have been able to write in Auschwitz? Shortly after they arrived on the train they would have been killed. How terrible it must have been; how often I think about it and mourn. It is so difficult to express how I feel, knowing that my parents whom I loved so much suffered in such a way. But I imagine that my brother's life in Auschwitz was a worse hell. Was living that torment better than dying right away?

At the end of the war we expected everyone to come back because we hadn't heard otherwise. We still didn't know what had happened to them. But soon after the war it all came out. Only a handful of people were left when, finally, the combined troops of the Allies liberated the concentration camps. Those still alive in these camps looked more like skeletons than living people. We all know now that the deported Jews and others of certain racial backgrounds, religious convictions and political leanings did not have a chance. But the Allies must have known what was happening in the concentration camps before the end of the war. I still don't understand why they didn't do something about it earlier. Could they not imagine how it was when children watched as their mothers and fathers were killed or how it was for the children and mothers as they were torn from each other, never to see each other again? From an inmate in Auschwitz, who had managed to stay alive till the end of the war and was freed by the Allied forces, my sisters and I heard that my brother Simon worked for two years before he died. This man told us that he and my brother lived together in the same barracks. Every morning at five o'clock they were driven outside where they worked for hours regardless of the weather. For two years my brother managed to stand the work until one morning he really could not get up. He had contracted typhus, as had so many other inmates. His friend who relayed the story said that when he returned to the barracks after work he had brought my brother something to eat, but his place was empty. What suffering Simon must have endured. He did not deserve this. He was such an agreeable, talented, loving person, and so young. Maybe I was granted my many years to be able to tell you about him and my other relatives who didn't survive.

Many people who came back after the war were scarred for life. Often they had been used as guinea pigs for all kinds of purposes. Many of the women who had experiments performed on them became sterile. This happened to the sister of my sister-in-law. She married some years after the war but could never have children. While some survivors suffered from bodily scars, many more would continue to be tormented by mental and emotional scars throughout their lives. As the years went by, mental disorders were common among survivors and many were institutionalized because of chronic depression and agonizing hallucinations about their ordeals in the concentration camps. For myself and other people I know, mental and emotional trauma seemed to develop later in life rather than right after the war. At the end of the war I was devastated when I learned of the deaths in my family, but I pushed aside the pain in order to keep functioning. I had my children to think about and I was just happy to be alive. Later on when the children grew up and I had more time, I started to think about it. And the younger generations began asking about what happened in the Holocaust. Like many other survivors who have lost family and friends, I would be lying to tell you that I no longer feel anger towards those who made and carried out the orders.

Although my husband Ernst and I did not experience the nightmare that befell our families, at times we have felt as though we had let our parents down. At the back of my mind I always feel the plaguing question — why? Why couldn't I save them? But in 1942 we knew only that all the Dutch Jews had to go to a different city, somewhere in Poland, where they would have to work in factories but could live in peace. They were told that things would be good, that they would be taken care of. It was all so early in the situation that no one suspected where events were heading. My parents' friends and family left full of optimism: "Maybe we'll see each other again. It will be fine." They all clung to hope. And what else could they do? With Hitler in power we had to follow the rules. If you didn't agree to go, they would come and get you. No one imagined that the Nazi regime would destroy them and so many others.

Now it all seems like a dream.

CHAPTER 2

Being Young

I was born Henriette Dwinger on August 26, 1918, in the town of Leeuwarden, the youngest child of my parents Kaatje and Joseph. My parents and grandparents on my mother's side, and generations before them had also lived in Leeuwarden, a small city in northern Holland's province of Friesland with a population of about fifty thousand. Leeuwarden had a large Jewish community. Like many other Jewish communities in Europe, they had formed their own settlement in the Middle Ages and lived as a kind of family in a special district or ghetto that was made up of a number of little streets built around the main building, the house of prayer, called the synagogue. The families were very religious and also very thankful to the monarchy in Holland for giving them the freedom to lead their own lives. They preserved their way of life by keeping to the law of God outlined in the Torah. Specifically, they formed their own customs in addition to the laws of the country, by keeping the Sabbath (Saturday) as their day of rest. Jewish stores were closed on this day. While outside the Jewish Quarter, business went on as usual, in this small community business stopped on this day: people went to the synagogue to pray, and for the remainder of the day they enjoyed a restful time together with their children and extended families. This day of rest gave everybody the strength to face another week of hard work.

We had a close relationship with my mother's side of the family because we all lived in the same city and my mother's family, the Cohens, were the backbone of our Jewish community. My grandfather, Benny, had six brothers who were all married to strong, healthy women rich in children. My mother had two sisters and three brothers. My grandfather, his six brothers, and all the extended family lived in the ghetto. Each brother had a little business. They all desired to have more for their children, especially for the boys, who later would have their own families. Together they owned a general store that their wives ran while each brother travelled out of the city, visiting farmers and selling his wares. They were not in competition with each other because every brother carried a different article for sale. Some sold hardware, some sold things such as curtains and drapes, wool, needles and cutlery. They walked for miles, either pushing a cart or a wheelbarrow, pulling a wagon, or carrying a backpack. As persistent as they were, they made sure to be back home by Friday afternoon, to bathe and dress themselves for the *Sjabbos* (Sabbath) dinner. But one thing still had to be done before they could serve God. They came together in one of their homes to put their profit on the table. They told each other how the week had gone and gave each other tips they had picked up about what the farmers wanted, so as to make sure, by their next visit, they would have this article with them. And the heap of money? It was counted and divided in seven equal amounts so that even if one of the brothers had not made much profit, he could have a restful *Sjabbos* and each of their wives could buy meat and baked goods. This way no one would be in a stressful situation. They trusted God would also approve. This happy family is always in my mind. Knowing where I came from, I try to live up to their image. I think of the many people who need help both in our own family as well as outside it, and I believe that in giving and helping them, the giver is actually happier than the receiver. To create a legacy after we are gone — this is what is required of us on earth.

My mother grew up in the Jewish Quarter. At that time women did not have a profession, but I know that she had worked in a studio where sheets and pillowcases were embroidered by hand. Only rich people could afford such items, of course. My mother must have earned a small salary for her embroidery. I still remember her making beautiful embroidered tablecloths and cushion tops. She was also very skilled in crocheting and knitting.

My father didn't come from Leeuwarden; he was from the nearby city of Groningen. He did not have a pleasant family life when he lived with his parents. His parents were poor and the family always looked to him for financial assistance, even after he married my mother. Of his three brothers, his youngest was mentally disabled. After his parents passed away and the two other brothers were married, my father took it upon himself to be a guardian of his handicapped brother. He made sure his brother lived with a capable family who looked after him. While this brother was able to do some manual work and earn a little, my parents would cover the rest of his expenses by sending a monthly cheque for his room and board. But sometimes he would get in trouble and we never knew when a phone call would come to tell us that he needed to be bailed out. I have the greatest respect for my father. He was the only one in his family to take on this serious responsibility. After my parents were gone, I don't know what happened to his brother. It could have been that he was sent away. Having been a nurse in a mental hospital, I know how much attention disabled people need, especially the mentally disabled, and how much such attention costs.

Marriages were mostly kept within the community, so many families were related to each other. I think my parents met at a dance held by the Jewish community in Leeuwarden. My father must have come just for the dance. I'm not sure how old my parents were when they married, probably in their early twenties. I believe they were married on the sixth of September 1904. They started having children right away. In fact, I suspect some hanky panky, since my brother Simon was born only seven months after they were married. Or perhaps he was just premature. I was the youngest child by far, nine years younger than my nearest sister, Johanna. My other sister Heintje was twelve and my brother Simon was fourteen when I was born.

I think I was a surprise to my parents, for I was born at a time when my mother no longer expected to have another child. She was already about forty years old and had recently recovered from a serious health problem after a miscarriage that had taken place a few years earlier when she was painting and wall-papering the living room and kitchen. Not having a stepladder, she used a stool to reach the ceiling. It must have been the worst stool in the house and not very sturdy. As she reached up, the leg of the stool collapsed and she fell and hit the edge of the wooden table. Since it did not hurt too much, she finished her job. After a few weeks she started to feel ill and realized that the baby wasn't moving anymore. She remembered how she had hit her stomach on the table when she fell. Her family doctor confirmed that the baby, a little boy, had died at that time.

But what could the doctor do now to help my mother? The baby had already begun to decompose and was poisoning her. In the early twentieth century, antibiotics had not yet been discovered as a means to combat infection, and the doctor could not operate because the flesh was infected and was thought not to heal afterwards. My mother was lucky; the doctor managed to get the baby out in pieces. It must have been terrible: the smell of decay would have been overpowering of course, but to see a precious little human removed in this way would have been heart-breaking. The doctor thought that my mother would be able to recover, but after several months she still did not feel well. So he advised her and my father to have another baby. He reasoned that the reproductive organs would not close up properly until my mother had another healthy delivery. My parents followed his advice, and voila! I came into the world as a necessity.

With my birth, my mother recovered and lived a relatively healthy life. But apparently I was a scrawny baby, perhaps because I was born after her miscarriage. I had big eyes and an ugly face, but my mother was so proud of me. When she took me to the men's clothing store that my Uncle Jan owned to show me off, he looked into the carriage and said, "Kaatje, you've got an ugly baby." My mother replied, "Drop dead!" and went home crying. Uncle Jan was the head of the family and a very opinionated, outspoken man. I remember once when I told him that I wanted to take bridge lessons with some of my girlfriends. He just looked at me and said, "You? You girl? You with your face? You'll never learn it!" And I never did. When I grew older I learned a lot from Uncle Jan. He always told the truth right away. I do too. I appreciated his honesty and still do. The truth was not always pleasant to hear but now, especially in my old age, I like honesty.

Uncle Jan could be infuriating with his honesty and his opinions, but he was also very generous. If my father was having a rough winter financially and we were hard pressed to get by till the summer, Uncle Jan would always lend my father some money. A small loan would usually get us through until my father could pay him back. Uncle Jan was also a real character and a bit of a joker. For example, his family always hired female housekeepers from Germany, as they tended to be hard-working and reliable. One particular housekeeper slept in the room next to his son's. Once, when my uncle went upstairs to see what they were doing, he discovered that his son had gone into the housekeeper's room. Uncle Jan didn't say anything but the next night he very carefully hung a pail of water over his son's door. When the son came out to sneak over to the girl's room the pail of water dropped on his head. He loved to tell such stories to the family. To be honest, I have clearer memories of him than I do of my own father, maybe because of his intense character. My father was not so extreme. After the war, however, Uncle Jan could not handle life anymore despite the strength of his character. He and his wife had gone into hiding and came back after the war. But neither of his two sons or their families returned after the Holocaust. Within a few years Uncle Jan became ill, and didn't live very long after. He died a broken man.

When I look back now, I consider my childhood in Leeuwarden to be a peaceful and happy one. The surrounding countryside in the province of Friesland was largely made up of farms. Potatoes and beets were farming staples but beans and carrots were also common. There was also quite a bit of dairy farming. Some farmers did both. It was a pleasant landscape. With its numerous lakes and rivers, many people spent their leisure time sailing and swimming. Many little canals ran through and around Leeuwarden. Some of the bigger canals had bridges that opened up to let the boats through. There were not any lakes in the city itself, but about ten miles out of the city there was a beautiful one. Actually it wasn't just one lake but many. We spent quite a bit of time there, swimming, rowing and relaxing. There was a substantial shopping district in Leeuwarden, and many professionals lived in the city. Amsterdam was about 130 kilometres away. Although it took only about two hours to reach there by train, I didn't go to Amsterdam until 1940 when I started training there as a nurse. But I'm jumping ahead of myself.

My parents were hardworking people and very loving. I saw their marriage as strong and stable. Perhaps by today's standards my mother's life would seem restrictive, since a wife was not considered equal to her husband at that time. There were no voting rights for women in Holland at the beginning of the twentieth century. A wife felt her place was mostly in the household. But my mother did not seem to mind. I remember her spending much of her time sitting by the window knitting, crocheting and sewing. She sewed most of our clothes.

My father was a good man and law-abiding, who had a job as a photographer. At a very young age, he had learned photography from his uncles and cousins. Many members of his family practised this trade. After my parents were married, he bought a house in the general business district. Located outside the Jewish sector of the city, my father's business was well known and respected by all. Before the war, few lines of distinction were drawn between Jews and non-Jews in terms of who supported whose business. In fact, our family, living outside the ghetto, was so integrated into the general Dutch community that on many occasions we didn't think ourselves so very different from the Dutch — that is, until the Nazis announced otherwise. Below our home was my father's store where we sold cameras and albums, and behind the store was a dark room that was separated from the hallway with two doors and from the workshop by another two doors. The double doors ensured that the dark room remained dark. He spent a lot of time developing pictures with another man who helped him. Behind the house was a simple wooden structure which he used as his studio. My father must have taken a thousand pictures of me, all of which went in the store window. Each time I would be wearing a different outfit!

Taking pictures was a serious business. If you look at the photos of the early twentieth century, everyone looks solemn or even surprised because, before he took their image, the photographer asked the subjects to look right into the camera and wait for the "little bird" to come out. At that time my father did not know about the saying, "say cheese," or any other way to encourage a more friendly expression on their faces. He was known among his colleagues as an excellent artistic photographer. Even the city magistrates engaged him to take pictures of buildings and structures. My father also had a contract to take school portraits in our province. At regular times, usually in intervals of three years, he visited each school. He would take photos of every class, showing the group of students, the teacher, and a sign held proudly by one of the students with the date and school year on it. In this way parents could buy a picture and keep a record of their child's development.

People often came to him to have their family portraits taken and he was regularly employed for weddings and other celebrations as well as in situations when someone was mortally ill. In the latter case, either the family would take this person to the studio or my father was called to the house. Cameras were not common or popular yet, so not everyone had one. If the family had no picture of the soon-to-be-departed member of the family, they would ask my father to come over and take one so that they could hang a framed picture on their wall as a memorial. Sometimes he'd get a phone call in the middle of the night asking him to come immediately to take a picture of the dying person. On more festive occasions he would often come home with the silliest stories. For instance, he had to take a wedding picture at the house of a bride where the whole family, including the bride and groom, was seated around a large table. In the center of the table was a large heap of unpeeled peanuts. Was this their wedding dinner? Reminiscing about these times, about the simplicity of everyday life and special occasions, still gives me a good feeling.

At the beginning of the twentieth century when the movie industry made headway in America, several members of my father's family emigrated to the United States to try their luck. They all succeeded, most of them living in Detroit where some of the first American films were produced. Later when the industry moved to California, they also moved. They wanted us to come over to America too, but my mother didn't want to go. At that point she had just had her miscarriage and was struggling to regain her health. And then there was the family. Most of her family lived in Leeuwarden and they were very close. No, my mother could not let go of her family ties. Imagine how different things could have been if we had gone. If I had known then what was to happen in Europe, that my parents and other family members would lose their lives in the Holocaust, I would have cried long and loud to make them know that I wanted to go to the United States. And maybe we would have gone. Our lives could have been so different.

My father was not particularly involved with my life. He was always busy and, to be honest, being the youngest, I didn't see him that much. In the summer he would have to work very hard to make up for the winter months, when he couldn't take pictures outside. My mother was much more available to me because she worked in the home. Occasionally she would help out at my father's store, but not often. She was not a business woman. Besides, keeping a house was a full-time job and a lot of work. My mother did all the cooking, and most of the washing, ironing and cleaning. We did have cold running water in the kitchen, which helped a bit. Other people had only one little tap in the hallway and would have to bring the water into the kitchen. House cleaning was labour intensive. I remember my mother on her knees sweeping the carpets with a brush and dustpan. It was a blessing when vacuums finally came on the market and she could buy one for a reasonable price. She also had a cleaning woman come in once a week for the rough work.

Toilets were sometimes the biggest mess. They were often located outside, behind the house in an open space. Since there was no toilet paper available, people would cut up old phone books and newspapers and hang the sheets on a hook in the outhouse. In this respect we were lucky, since we had a little room with a toilet inside the house. It was a built-in shelf with a hole and a lid. Underneath was a very visible metal barrel used for holding the waste, which would be collected twice a week. A barge would arrive (we lived on a canal) and the barrels were taken away and traded for fresh, clean, empty ones. I distinctly remember one occasion when the man who usually came to our house to change the barrels lost his footing on our stairs. It is not necessary to describe the mess and stink that resulted. I'm not sure how they cleaned it up because I slipped out of the house. When I came back a couple of hours later, all was cleaned up but not completely odour free. It took quite some time before the smell finally disappeared.

Once a week a tall, stern, angry looking woman named Marijke came to the house to wash, starch and iron my father's shirts. The collars were so stiff that my mother could not finish the shirts, no matter how much she tried. Marijke never talked, she received a couple of coins for her work, and left with the next bundle of shirts. On one occasion, however, I remember somebody in the family had a birthday and my mother invited her to stay and have a cup of coffee with us. My mother was welcoming to everybody, and I think she was anxious to know why this woman was so stolid and unfriendly. After a time, she encouraged Marijke to talk and it was indeed a sad story. She had never married, and from the age of twenty she had cleaned and ironed shirts for people. It turned out she really hated the work. For the first time in her drab life she started to cry and pour out her heart. After this episode my mother understood Marijke better, and they often drank a cup of coffee together.

Cooking was also a complicated task. To make simple coffee my mother would have to grind the beans and then cook them on a small oil burner. We had electricity only for lighting. Breakfast was a pleasure but not without a lot of effort. Not many people owned a toaster. If someone was lucky enough to have one, it was the kind where someone would have to watch the bread constantly so it would not burn to a crisp. Nor did we have a refrigerator, and consequently my mother often had to throw out food and milk. And we couldn't just go to a supermarket and pick up pre-cooked products, canned goods or frozen foods. Most ingredients had to be prepared at home. For Friday's *Sjabbos* dinner, my mother would begin preparations on Thursday night. She would put an old newspaper on the table, a chicken and a couple of knives. She had to clean the chicken completely, inside and out. The innards, such as the lungs and kidneys, would have to come out. She even had to pluck some of the feathers that were forgotten by the slaughterhouse. On Friday it took all day to clean the vegetables and cook the *Sjabbos* meal. The cooking was often done on one or more oil burners. You had to watch these burners constantly because without warning they turned themselves up and the food would burn. Or, a little draft could blow out the flame and the food would not be ready on time.

On other evenings after our light supper of sandwiches, my mother would do the dishes in the back of the kitchen. Because I was the youngest, I didn't have to do any family chores. At least I don't remember doing any. I think I must have been quite a spoiled child. But I do remember cleaning off the table once. I was supposed to take the tablecloth to the back of the house and shake it out outside. And I was so stupid that I came into the kitchen with the tablecloth and asked, "Where am I supposed to shake this out?" As a joke Johanna replied, "Oh, just do it here." And I dropped one end of the table cloth, throwing all the crumbs on the floor. Everyone laughed.

Of my three siblings, I was closest to my sister Jo at this period, probably because she was the nearest to me in age, even though she was nine years older. Jo was my confidante. I was her little sister. We slept in the same bed, which was so small that we could hardly turn around. In the winter it was often icy cold. Our pot-belly stove or hearth heated only one room, the family room. Because the room and bed were so cold, I didn't like to go to bed. And I didn't want to get up either, because at night, under the heavy woollen blankets with a hot water bottle for your feet, the cold was bearable. Stepping on the icy floor in the morning with my bare feet was no pleasure. When it was really cold, the water in the wash basin would freeze, and to wash up I would have to break the thin layer of ice.

While I looked up to Jo with great admiration, I am sure there were times when she must have come close to hating me, especially when my mother said to her, "Listen Jo, you have to look after her, eh?" She would respond, "Yah, I'll do it," but her friends would be playing outside and she'd want to play with them, and I was only a baby. Once, when I was really young, she sat me by the window and said, "Okay, put your one arm here and the other arm along the window sill and sit like this until I come back." I sat still like that for an hour while she was playing outside. When my mother found me like that, Jo caught hell!

Heintje was my other sister. She thought her name was unfortunate because it was so old-fashioned. At that time, parents often named their children after their grandparents, so that's how she ended up with her name. She changed it to Henny. When I was a kid she would take me skating and swimming. Since there were no swimming pools, I learned how to swim in a lake and eventually was very good at it. I could swim under water for at least twenty meters. When I'd do it, Henny would yell her head off, "Ahhhh! My sister is drowning, someone go help her!" They'd all come running and then my head would pop up far in the distance and I'd wave hello. Once we were older, I probably grew closer to Henny than to Jo in some ways. I could always go to her if I had a problem. Henny was more down to earth, while Jo carried herself in a more sophisticated manner. Henny and Johanna also grew closer when they were older, especially when Henny became a widow. She would often stop in at Jo's for a cup of coffee after shopping, as they lived in the same city.

I didn't get to know Simon in the same way as my sisters. Since he was fourteen years older than I was, he was basically out of the house by the time I really remember anything. But I do remember that for my ninth or tenth birthday, he gave me a beautiful little ring. Since he could not be home for my birthday that year, he gave my mother money to buy a ring for me. She went to the jewellery shop down the street and bought a gold ring with a little mother of pearl stone inset in it. I wore it all the time. It was so special to me because I could wear it every day and think of him every time I looked down at my hand. Finally, when my fingers grew bigger and I could no longer wear it, it had to be kept safely in a little box.

When he still lived in Leeuwarden, he married a lovely woman named Esther, and they had twins, a boy and a girl. I really enjoyed spending time with the twins. My sister-in-law invited me over almost every Thursday night while I was in high school. My brother was often not in town because he was a photography salesman affiliated with Kodak and would be away for a few days at a time. She would make a special dinner that I really enjoyed and then we would spend time chatting together and playing with the twins. It is a terrible shame that Simon, Esther and I did not have the opportunity to know each other as adults because I was only in my early twenties when they were deported. And their twins did not even live to see adulthood.

In our home all four of us children played an instrument. My oldest brother Simon played the violin. He was very talented, a real prodigy. We called him wonder child. He played so well as a child of five or six years old that he played in an orchestra with adults. My two sisters, Henny and Jo, played the piano. I also played the violin, but my abilities were only average. All those lessons must have cost our parents a fortune. My mother had high aspirations for me, hoping that I would become a violinist and learn the xylophone. But I wanted to be a movie star; I wanted to be in show business. I would stare in the mirror for hours making all kinds of different faces. I wanted to be like Sylvia Sydney, Betty Davis or Clara Bo, whose pictures I plastered all over my wall. I also liked Laurel and Hardy. As a photographer, my father was able to get home movies to show the family. We'd put the projector on the table and someone would have to crank it the whole time so we could see. I remember watching Charlie Chaplin that way. And later on when I was older, maybe about sixteen or seventeen, I became part of an amateur acting group. We had a Jewish acting club in Leeuwarden and twice a year we would put on a show for the Jewish community. Since my sister Jo and I both loved acting, we became involved when I was in my teens. The plays tended to be simple with a happy ending. Definitely not the stuff of Shakespeare but very enjoyable to perform.

Despite my love of acting and desire to be in the limelight, I was generally a quiet, contented child who liked to be alone and read. I was a real bookworm when I was young. I think my favourite book was *Rebecca*. I would often go to the library to sign out books, but the city library was small. It was probably no bigger than my kitchen here so there were not all that many books that I could borrow. If it was my birthday, everyone brought books for me as gifts because they knew how much I liked reading. For special events, such as birthdays, the whole family gathered together for a big celebration. Some family members brought a few books and asked me to choose one. Stores allowed people to do that, and then the customer would bring back the ones they didn't want. I would turn invisible then. I'd sneak up to my bedroom during the party so that I could begin my new books. I also liked to write stories. When I was a young girl of ten or eleven years I often wrote little narratives for a small Jewish newspaper in Leeuwarden. They were always stories with happy endings. Maybe I should have been a writer, but my parents didn't really know how to encourage me in this field or have the money to give me a higher education.

My school years were rather uneventful. My grade school was a distinguished Dutch private girls' school of about two hundred students, largely girls from well-to-do families. Each grade was separate, with about twenty students in a class, and only one class per grade. All my siblings had gone to public school but, as the youngest child, I was singled out for special schooling. Perhaps my parents had a bit more money by this time, and were able to enrol me in private school. I think my parents did whatever they could to improve our image and make sure that we would be popular among our friends. Personally, I would have preferred to have boys and girls together and would not have minded going to a public school at all. On our school ground there was another building that housed the all-boys' school. As we had our recess breaks at different times we could never play together.

Our uniform consisted of a kind of beret, but we could wear whatever we wanted for the rest of our outfit. My mother made all my clothes and knitted sweaters for all of us. Nobody ever noticed that a dress from one of my older sisters was done over. As a Jewish girl I was not in the popular crowd and neither were the other Jewish pupils. There were a few Jewish girls in each class of largely Dutch students. Sometimes we would feel as though we were not part of the group and kept to ourselves. Nonetheless, I don't remember feeling particularly isolated. I had Dutch friends at

school. One of them was Gretel, whose father owned a candy factory. At the end of the week when the workers received their pay
checks they would always be given a small bag of candy. My friends
and I would stand by the factory gate to get some as well. Gretel's
family was wealthy and lived in what seemed to me a very large
house, but they were not frivolous or showy with their money. In
fact, when Gretel was given a new dress, it was a big deal, certainly
not an every-day occurrence. She was really nice to me, whereas
some of the other girls could be snooty.

If you did not appear at school every day your parents would
receive a letter, and if you were absent longer the police would
come. Parents were required to give a valid excuse; otherwise the
father could be arrested. Every now and then I skipped a day, but
my parents knew about it and didn't mind. My day off school was
not really a waste because I needed it to relax and be quiet. My
mother would even make my favourite food. After this day off, I
would be okay for a few months. Once a year we would have an
official day off, a kind of play day, where we would spend the day
outdoors in the park and have a picnic together as a class. It was
the real highlight of the school year.

My best subject was arithmetic, but I enjoyed writing too. Generally, though, I was an average student. There are two teachers
from grade school that stand out in my mind. One of them, Miss
Hookstra, pulled students by the hair when they didn't want to listen. That was in grade four and five. In Holland at that time it was
common for teachers to accompany their classes for a number of
grades. I was thrilled when I was finally liberated from Miss Hookstra's tutelage. The teacher that I really liked was Miss Heuvel. She
was a very friendly lady. She had a camera and often came to our
store to get her pictures developed.

In school I didn't notice the anti-Semitism that much. But in
the neighbourhood, things were a little bit different. I was good
friends with the neighbourhood children who were mostly Dutch.
We would go bike riding, play at skipping or *knikkeren* (marbles).
For marbles we'd make a little hole in the ground, sit about six-

teen in a row, and try to throw the marbles into the hole. Whoever got the most marbles in the hole or closest to the hole was the winner. We'd also play hide and seek, and a kind of game where we would juggle three balls against the wall. I think my favourite game, though, was ringing the doorbells on other people's houses and then running away. I was a real tomboy, always fighting with the boys. But if I ever got in a fight on the street or got in a tiff with one of my girlfriends, it was always, "Dirty Jew." I thought it was my middle name. I remember looking down at my dress thinking, "But I'm not dirty, I'm clean!" I couldn't understand what they meant. I also noticed that when non-Jewish children came to my house, they were invited inside our living room, but I don't remember being invited into their homes, as I was with my Jewish friends. I would have to play outside with them. I think we felt that the anti-Semitism was there, but we lived with it. No one expected that being Jewish would turn out to be such a catastrophic thing. In fact, I don't really remember experiencing strong anti-Semitism until the Nazis came in and set up all kinds of rules against us.

Although being Jewish was a big part of my life, I didn't think too much about my Jewish identity. It wasn't something that I thought to tell people or talk about. My mother kept up many of the Jewish religious traditions that she had learned as a child. Like her extended family, most of the Jews in the Leeuwarden community were Orthodox and very religious. Our family would have considered themselves Orthodox. My parents were upstanding members of the Jewish community, but at the same time they did not practise religion excessively. We went to synagogue regularly every other week and held the Sabbath. We also ate kosher, keeping dishes and utensils separate in our house (milk dishes apart from the meat dishes). My mother was an upstanding Jewish woman and I remember that on *Sjabbos* we were not allowed to colour or write on paper. While the schools were open on this day and other pupils attended classes, I had my school work sent home, and on Sunday I had to study. I did not always like it, but that is how things were.

To prepare for *Sjabbos*, on Friday afternoons I would have my bath in a small wash basin filled with warm water on the floor of my bedroom. I remember my mother would wash my back; the rest I could reach for myself. I felt so clean afterwards, and after a change of underwear it was as though I were on top of the world. This ceremony only happened once a week, so on *Sjabbos* I would parade around wearing my best dress and fancy hat down the street or in the park later that evening. I would meet my girl-friends there and sometimes boys too.

On *Sjabbos* most of the Jewish stores were closed so many of us would visit in the park. There were two major parks in Leeuwarden: Prinsentuin and Rengers Park. We would frequently gather to-gether in Prinsentuin. Or sometimes some of my relatives would walk over to visit over a glass of Schnapps. We practised the Jewish religion but did not practise all the religious particulars. For in-stance, we kept the Sabbath but didn't light candles for the meal as more Orthodox Jews would have done. And my father had his photography store open on Saturdays just like any other day. We were rather free with our religion. We also didn't celebrate all the annual holidays. We did celebrate Passover, though, together as an extended family. We would go to my uncle's house for Passover. As he had a good voice and knew the Torah, he'd do the reading for us. And we would light candles every evening for Hanukkah.

On Sunday mornings and Wednesday afternoons I went to a special Hebrew school for about an hour or so. We learned the traditional Jewish stories from the Torah about God and the his-tory of Jews in the world. I don't remember thinking much about God except as "something" for which I needed to have respect. God saw everything. I didn't think about God much as a child, nor do I remember my parents talking much about God. God was a spirit you didn't see. You knew you had to be good. It was similar to when I saw a policeman on the road when I was young. I would walk very carefully and properly. I thought of God as a very pow-erful policeman. The Hebrew school itself was run by the Jewish community. It had two rooms, and when you were promoted you moved from one room to the other. I think I stopped by the time I went to high school.

As if I didn't have enough of girls in grade school, my high school was also an all-girls' school, and again there was another high school for the boys. We would have dance parties periodically in which the boys from the boys' school would invite girls from our school. But I had trouble with that. Being Jewish, I'd need to have a Jewish date. And none of the Jewish boys that I knew wore long pants. In Holland they all wore shorts, summer and winter. I could never find a boy who wore long pants. And you can't go to a dance with someone wearing shorts or who didn't have a whole suit. But perhaps that was just my excuse. At any rate I could never find a partner for those dances. I never went to many of the parties, either. I think I would have liked to go, but if you cannot find anyone to go with, what can you do?

One thing I did do was to attend other dances that were held outside the school. There was a great dance hall in town with windows all around and even some entertainment. We had some real dancers there, some ladies or couples. Sometimes a magician would also perform. It had a proper dance floor, a restaurant and tables and chairs where we could sit and have a drink or something to eat. That was a popular spot to meet someone. The boys were very well behaved. They didn't go around and grab girls in public; you just didn't do that sort of thing. Nor did you openly show affection. Maybe holding hands, but that would be all. Nor did boys want or expect anything sexual from a girl right away in order to satisfy themselves. At least that's not how they came across. I dated a few Jewish boys as a teenager. You could go to the movies on a date for very little — perhaps ten or twenty cents, in Canadian money. Now and then we'd go to the theatre. Or you could take a walk and sit in the park. I don't remember going out for dinner on a date or even going out to dinner with my parents for that matter. Needless to say, we did not even consider dating a Dutch boy.

A young person under the age of sixteen years was not allowed in the workforce, not even for a summer job. We had to go to school until we reached working age. Following my school years in the 1930s, I worked in a lingerie store for a year. At this time the first brassieres came out that really showed off more of your figure. I got my first bra there. It made me look as though I actually had breasts. As I was young and pretty, I was the first employee chosen to wear one, which I did to show the potential customers how it would look.

Up until then, we girls had to wear rugged knitted cotton stockings and a girdle to hold them up, together with a straight piece of elastic that went around our chests. This combination of girdle and "brassiere" was called a corselet. I wore a camisole underneath it. The corselet did up at the side. It was made of stiff uncomfortable material, and after a while it would start to stink. It was really uncomfortable to wear in the hot summer (fortunately Holland isn't a hot country). When I think about it now, I shudder. I still remember the stiff corsets with drawstrings in the back. How could we breathe? And then there was the wasp waistline that my mother practised. In the mornings I watched her in her bedroom strapping herself in so she would look good. What nonsense we went through just to look pretty. Men had to wear a high shirt collar and stiff shirts full of starch, but somehow that didn't seem to compare. In the twenties and thirties the dress style became somewhat looser but the women still did not show much of their shape.

When I think back now at what we used to wear, I realize that we did not own many clothes, although at the time it seemed quite natural that even underwear was scarce. Usually we had one set on the body, one in the wash, and one set on the shelf if you needed a change in between bath days. And when we had our periods, it was even worse. We would use a kind of bandage, a long strip of cloth with the consistency of a thick towel. Or sometimes a thin towel folded a couple of times. Of course they would have to be washed. Beside our kitchen we had a little enclave or storage room where we had a pail under a table. With three girls at home, there were always bandages in there. These bandages would not protect you from leaking, so during our periods we would buy rubber pants to wear over our underpants in case of leakage. For cramps we could take aspirin, but there wasn't much else available for the pain. A hot water bottle was the best medication. It was all part of what a woman had to suffer in that time.

After my job in the lingerie store, I found a position in the office of a shoe factory where I earned thirty-five guilders a month. This so-called office was where they showed off the shoe samples. As my feet were pretty small I would model the samples to demonstrate the new shoes. At the time, such jobs were all I could find. Not many young people went on for higher education after high school. A university education was reserved for the rich people who could afford it. Nor were there very many options open to girls. Most girls just wanted to be married and have a family. If someone was really outstanding at their schoolwork, the schoolteacher would come to the student's house and suggest to the parents that she be allowed to continue her studies. Sometimes the government would help these students financially. But generally speaking, if a young woman needed or wanted a job, she could become a clerk in a store or office, a nurse, a cleaning lady, or she could work in a factory. My sister Johanna became a lab technician, which was not a common profession for a woman. Although the lab technician courses were not as extensive as today's, they took considerable effort and you had to be quite studious to receive the diploma. After the course, Jo finished off her training by working in the laboratory. If I remember correctly, it was a cheese and butter factory, mostly employing men.

The mid-1930s offered new fashion and job opportunities for women, as well as a general boost to the economy. Especially in Germany. In 1933 Hitler was appointed chancellor with the assistance of the aging and somewhat senile President Paul von Hindenburg. Hitler turned the German economy around and began to bolster German national pride. But to bring Germany to a state of Aryan glory, the Jews would have to disappear. The rest is history. And what a history. In Holland, a sister party called the N.S.B., or

National Socialist Movement (*Nationaal Socialistische Beweging*), embraced similar ideals to those of the Nazi party in Germany, preaching the same excessive sermons that Hitler preached to the Germans. In fact, the N.S.B. had been formed in Holland several years before Hitler came to power in Germany. Since Holland was a democracy, the N.S.B. had the right to try to influence the people by means of rallies, hate mail, newspaper articles and so on. Initially, most Dutch people just made jokes about them. It was such a small party that it did not seem strong enough to make trouble. We knew they were there, but we thought they were ineffectual. In Leeuwarden they met in a small plain house. What could we possibly have to fear?

Apparently more than we could have imagined. The N.S.B. continually gained more members who seemed ready to do anything for the progress of the party. The underlying anti-Semitism that we had lived with and tried to ignore gradually began to increase. Little by little, Jewish stores lost customers and finally their livelihood. Many Jewish families began needing financial assistance, but the Dutch government could not or would not come to their aid. Well-to-do Jewish families helped out until finally they also had to be careful not to go broke themselves. Among the people who later needed financial help were my parents. Other photographers, those who were in accord with the new movement, competed for the important jobs. Although my father was one of the best and previously one of the most respected, he couldn't get much work. Even neighbours who would earlier have come over for a friendly little talk began to stay away. We were surprised and wondered where this new anti-Jewish behaviour would lead. We assumed it was just a passing phase.

CHAPTER 3

Nathan

Before the war and the Holocaust started in Europe, the anti-Semitism we suffered in Holland was already present in Germany, but with much greater intensity. Long before 1940, Jewish people in Germany were being persecuted. Even before Hitler's rise to power in 1933, his National Socialist party (Nazis) discriminated against the Jewish population with obscene language and random beatings. After Hitler was made chancellor of Germany, the anti-Semitism became more organized and methodical. In September 1935, the Nuremberg Laws were put into effect. They stated that people with Jewish ancestry (meaning those with at least one Jewish grandparent) were not allowed to marry or have sexual relations with an "Aryan." They also stripped Jews of their German citizenship. A few months later, Jews who were employed as civil servants began to be dismissed. The plan was to have no Jews left in the government, in professional positions or in cultural life by 1938. Then, in the summer of 1938, Jews in Germany had to carry special papers that identified them as Jews. But somehow these acts of discrimination seemed tolerable compared to the blatant hatred demonstrated in the *Kristallnacht* (The Night of Broken Glass) on November 9 and 10, 1938. On these nights stores, houses and synagogues were destroyed and many Jews were arrested. Finally the German Jews began to realize that, despite their hopes for peace and their desire to maintain some semblance of ordinary life in their homes and communities, Germany was not a safe place. But by this time it was very difficult to emigrate, unless the family had a lot of money. Most Jews in Germany were already doomed.

One of those was a young German Jew from Essen, Germany, whom I befriended around this time. His name was Nathan Grüner. I saw him for the first time at my sister Johanna's bakery in 1934. Johanna and her husband Bram owned a Jewish bakery in Winterswijk, a Dutch town close to the German border. During that time people from Germany often came over to buy their Jewish pastry. Everything was kosher. Religious travellers, vacationers or local shoppers who bought pastry often rested in the annex, a little eating area attached to the bakery that had three small tables for lunches. Here they could buy coffee, tea or other drinks to have alongside their fresh pastry. One day Nathan came in with his mother, bought pastry and had some coffee in the annex. Because my sister had just had her first baby, Joop, I was at the bakery to help, so I served Nathan and Mrs. Grüner. Since it wasn't very busy we struck up a conversation and I sat down with them. He didn't speak much Dutch, being from Germany, so we spoke German together. In Holland we had to learn German in school, so I knew it quite well. He continued to come regularly, and when I wasn't occupied in the bakery I would sit and talk with him. I think he was interested in me, but I didn't like him right away. I was only sixteen at the time and he was eleven years older. Not that I minded the age difference. You couldn't tell by looking at him, and I don't think I even realized the age gap initially. I thought that he was a good-looking fellow — about five feet, nine inches, with dark wavy hair and brown eyes. But I was not seriously looking to begin a relationship. Even so, we started corresponding with each other by letter. That was in 1935.

Nathan was living with his widowed mother, and together they operated a furniture store. The family also had a photo-finishing shop. His father had died in 1919 when he and his two brothers, Julius and Joseph, were still very young. Since the other two boys were studying, Nathan stayed with his mother to help in the store. When the store was taken over and closed by the Nazis in 1936, he and his mother had to live on their savings. For a couple of years we corresponded. Then he stopped writing, for his life in Germany had become difficult. Later in 1938, after *Kristallnacht*, he suddenly fled to Holland where he made contact with me. Unfortunately for him and for us, he had not come to Holland of his free will; he was fleeing the Gestapo. I never did find out why they were searching for him. People at that time were arrested in Germany on the slightest pretence, and of course he was Jewish.

Since Nathan needed money and somewhere to stay, I found him a place with a family and managed to get him a weekly or monthly allowance from the Jewish Committee in the city. He also tried to work a little. He became a handy-man, having learned to make furniture through the family business in the furniture store. He rented a small space and made small tables. In the late 1930s, Hitler wasn't in power yet in Holland so a few people were still giving Jews some of their business. At the family's house he had his own room where he cooked a little for himself, buying food-stuffs with money he received from the Jewish community. I can still see him sitting by his little table in his attic room with a piece of bread on the table and a bit of butter and cheese. He was very simple in his culinary tastes, and since he couldn't buy very much food, he lost a fair bit of weight. His mother came to see him occasionally. She was an elegant petite lady, very friendly and appreciative that my family and I took an interest in his situation. Nathan stayed, and I grew to love him. My parents did not want me to become too close to him, especially because he was so much older than I was. But who listens to their parents? I don't remember having outright fights with them about him, but I know that they really didn't approve of the situation.

In 1940 I decided to go into nursing and became a student nurse. Nursing was not necessarily a profession for which I had a natural inclination, but I had a good friend in high school who had wanted to be a nurse and enjoyed the profession. So I reasoned, if she likes it, I might like it too. There was a rule that required student nurses to be at least twenty before they began their studies. Being now just over twenty years old, I moved to Amsterdam to begin my schooling in a private Jewish hospital there. At that time nursing students didn't go to university but would receive lessons right in the hospital while assisting other nurses. We would even get a little money while we were training, about fifteen guilders a month. The full schooling would take about three years. Because the hospital was Jewish I did not experience anti-Semitism among the staff. In fact, the hospital was not segregated according to race at all; the doctors were so well respected that non-Jews often sought treatment there.

I lived at the hospital in a nurses' residence where all the nurses had to live, not just the students. We were able to see our family and friends on our days off, usually a couple of days every other week. Occasionally I was able to visit my brother Simon and his family. They had moved from Leeuwarden to Hilversum, which was only about a fifteen-minute train ride from Amsterdam. Despite our age difference, I enjoyed visiting him and his family. Like all young people, I was very busy. In addition to studying and nursing, I had a lot of fun with my co-workers, going out, and making every minute count. Right beside the hospital was a zoo with a large grassy park area. Some of the other nurses and I were such regular attendees at the zoo that we decided to become members. We would often head next door for our lunch breaks, buy ourselves ice-cream for dessert and sit on the benches in the sun, soaking up the lovely surroundings. After living in a smaller community for my whole life, I enjoyed the bustle and activity of Amsterdam.

When I went into nursing, Nathan followed me to Amsterdam and we continued our relationship. We got along quite well, although I did feel the age gap at times. He was a rather critical thinker and always knew better than I did. But he was also generous. I remember he bought me a little gold watch to hang from my shirt, a very fashionable thing at the time. And he was really funny. There was a Shirley Temple movie that was popular while we were together, and he'd sing, "On the good ship lollipop, la la la la la." It was so humorous because he didn't know English at all, and there he was trying to sing this silly English song. We laughed a lot. We weren't able to see each other often, since we could only spend time together on my days off; the time we had together was spent going for walks and hanging out in cafes. We could still do those sorts of things before 1941. Because he didn't really have any money, it was hard to go out and do something exciting or costly. Although things weren't going well for him at that time, he always had hope that the situation would improve. Besides, we didn't need money to enjoy each other's company.

Considering our love for each other, the outcome is not difficult to imagine. But it did come as a shock. I became pregnant. It was a jolt for both of us, of course. Nathan tried to be supportive, but it was impossible for him to marry me because he was a fugitive German Jew in hiding. Knowing that he was not a completely free man, I did not demand marriage. Essentially, I was on my own. I tried to hide the fact that I was pregnant and continued working in the hospital. Since getting pregnant without being married was really taboo, I knew I would be asked to leave the hospital where I was undertaking my student training if they found out. I didn't eat very much and took a laxative every day to try and get rid of any extra fat, so I didn't look much bigger. On the day I went into labour, I got up in the morning and thought, "Oh my god, I'm in such pain." I had no idea what giving birth was like. I hobbled to the bathroom and my water broke. But I didn't know what to do.

I decided to try and continue with my nursing duties. Somehow I managed till twelve o'clock when we had an hour off for lunch. At noon I left the hospital, stepped onto a streetcar, went to another hospital and had my baby. Naturally I didn't come back to work in the afternoon. The staff at this hospital had to inform the hospital where I was working that I was giving birth. Nobody could believe it; I had hidden it so well the whole nine months. My first daughter, Elly, was born in September 1940. She wasn't even that small when she was born — six pounds and healthy.

After Elly's birth I didn't go home with her because my father and mother could not accept that I had had a baby. Being pregnant without a husband was a real disgrace in those days. And my parents were ashamed. What would people think? They worried that the extended family, especially, would look down on me. In actuality, the family responded with mixed reactions. On the one hand they were ashamed of me, and on the other hand they felt sorry for me and looked on me with compassion. For them, it was "all *his* fault," and they were more upset with him than with me. Maybe it was partially his fault. He was eleven years older and should have known what he was doing. I was just a kid, only twenty. I had never been seriously involved with anyone before him and knew nothing about having a sexual relationship or taking precautions. Then there was that agonizing thought in the back of my mind that he must have known more girls in Germany and that maybe I was only a substitute for the time that he was in Holland. Did he really mean for me to be his wife? We loved each other, but would this have been enough to raise a child? Without jobs or money? So many questions.

In the midst of my personal changes, the political and social scene in Holland shifted dramatically. Despite the fact that Germany had annexed Austria in 1938 and conquered Poland in 1939, we hoped the German political and anti-Semitic storm clouds would not affect us directly. But in May 1940, when I was still pregnant with Elly and working in the Jewish hospital in Amsterdam, the clouds gathered over Holland and burst open. A little party for my mother's sixtieth birthday had been organized, and I was planning to go home for it. At that time my mother was living with my older sister Henny, her husband Arnold, and their two girls in Amersfoort. My parents had been forced to give up their home in Leeuwarden because they had very little business, and they couldn't afford to own a house anymore. Initially they kept it but rented it out. My father stayed in Leeuwarden because he could still make a bit of money, but he was forced to rent a small room in another house. My sister Jo and her family were living with Henny as well. Jo and Bram had lost their bakery in Winterswijk around 1938. Jewish people were not coming anymore, especially those from Germany. A number of Jews were emigrating to England or to the States at that time. The ones who had a lot of money and foresight tried to get out of Holland and Germany if they still could. Those who remained didn't have much money and were not about to spend what little they had on nonessentials like pastry. Since none of them were doing well financially, both of my sisters, their families, and my mother lived together. Eking out an existence was more possible that way.

I had not forgotten about my mother's birthday, but all of a sudden it was there — only two days away — and I had not asked for a leave of absence. When I asked for a few days off, my request was refused. The schedules were already made up, and even though my work was not too important (passing bedpans around, folding gauze, etc.), I was told I was needed. Of course I complained to the other nurses and felt especially hard done by when I was also put on the night shift. In fact, night shift was not really that bad since it was usually much quieter than day shift. In truth, I liked the quiet. Thinking about this now, I was probably just feeling sorry for myself that I had not been allowed to visit my mother on her birthday.

Anyway, late at night on May 9, 1940, I was working with another student nurse in the little kitchen on the third floor of our hospital, making a snack for us. It was twelve thirty, shortly after midnight, when all of a sudden there was a thunderous crash and instantly all the lights went out. My heart was pounding as we found our way to the fourth floor, where the operating rooms and the laboratories were. We thought that perhaps somebody had left some chemicals or equipment unattended. We could not open the doors nor could we see very much. Moonlight was our only light, which made us realize that the streetlights were all off, and that the crashes and explosion had come from different directions. We ran down to the third floor to find it in total chaos. Some patients were ringing their bed bells, others were hysterical. All were shouting questions that we could not answer. Other nurses from daytime staff, half-asleep and half-dressed, came to help. Interns appeared on the scene. We were all scared but our first duty was to help the people back in their beds and calm them down.

Soon a generator was started up and the lights came back on. Meanwhile, there was more crashing, bombing and shooting all around us. And then we understood. Through the windows in the dark street we noticed things coming down, hundreds of objects falling from the sky. When they came close enough we could see that they were parachutes carrying people and equipment. They landed right in Amsterdam, even in our street. This all lasted for several hours, and when it finally quieted down we realized that Amsterdam had fallen to the Germans. When morning finally came, tanks rolled in. This was the beginning of a five-year Dutch hell under German occupation. Transportation was completely cut off; nobody could leave the city. For us, the war started on my mother's sixtieth birthday in 1940, and it would be more than three months before I was able to see her again.

A few days later, Holland's port city, Rotterdam, was overtaken by the Germans. They came in with their ships, bombed the harbour, and flattened over half of it. Jo's husband Bram was called up for duty to fight the Germans in Rotterdam. Apparently he was in the train station between sandbags when they bombed the station, levelling it. He was the only one in the station who survived because he was protected by those sandbags. But when they pulled him out they saw that his leg was completely damaged. He had been buried for a couple of days under rubble, and the wounds in his leg had become so seriously infected that they could not save his limb. It was amputated just above the knee. Not only did he lose his leg, but his hip never completely healed. His ribs and his arms had been broken too. The worst part was that his brain had also suffered because of a very high fever, and for the rest of his life he spoke in a much more measured manner when trying to express himself. He was taken to the hospital where he stayed for more than two years recuperating. About eight hundred people died in the German bombings of Rotterdam and almost eighty thousand Dutch residents were left homeless. With this major defeat, the Dutch army officially surrendered to the Germans.

For those of us in Amsterdam, at daybreak after the parachutes had landed, we awoke to see the new flags — red and black German flags and banners with the swastika emblem, waving from the official buildings, on the lawns, out the windows, from the rooftops, wherever possible. I was sorry to see that they also flew from quite a large number of private Dutch homes. Private citizens were obviously hoping that early co-operation could save their lives; displaying Nazi flags seemed to them the best way to prevent trouble. They were not necessarily pro-German, just cautious. To me, this was a sign of weak character. For while young men and women were being pulled off the streets because of their resistance, these cowards were sitting home behind their safe doors and windows.

Initially we did not feel the oppression, as daily activities carried on relatively undisturbed. Life also went on as normal in the Jewish hospital where I worked. Trains, streetcars and general traffic began moving again and most people, including Jews, thought that whatever they had read about the Hitler regime had been blown out of proportion. It might not be that bad after all. Life was bearable and when help finally came from England, which it surely would, it would be over. Holland would be Holland again. But this was not how it went. In a mere four days, the Germans had overrun Holland. Belgium and France were defeated shortly thereafter, much to our shock. France's famous defence strategy based on the Maginot Line (a concentration of all their forces along one long trench in case of German invasion) failed miserably. The Germans just bypassed it. Soon we heard that the German Army was in the streets of Calais, holding a large body of British and French soldiers trapped against the coast of the Franco-Belgian border at Dunkirk and waiting for instructions to cross over to England. In the meantime, England sent out ships of all kinds to evacuate the trapped Allied soldiers and succeeded in rescuing over three hundred and thirty thousand of them. Even though the soldiers escaped, they were ill-equipped to help the countries which had surrendered, at least for the moment anyway.

Everything happened so quickly. Less than two years earlier, on September 30, 1938, Prime Minister Neville Chamberlain of England had just returned from Germany where he had met with Hitler. Hitler had promised him and the world, too, of course, that Germany had no intentions of conquering Europe. His plan was to assimilate Austria and the other countries which, according to official Nazi doctrine, had at one time belonged to Germany. Having been assured that Germany would never attack the rest of Europe and that their aggression would end with Czechoslovakia and Austria, the English military machine had not prepared for war. England had a huge navy, but their lack of land forces meant they were not ready for war. They had enough men but insufficient armaments as the battle of Dunkirk revealed all too well. From this time on, England did everything they could to ready their equipment, army and air force in order to stave off German invasion. If England had fallen, Germany would soon have conquered most of Europe. Fortunately, at this crucial point, the war had taken a disappointing turn for Germany.

Nonetheless, whatever political disappointments Nazi Germany faced with England at that time did not change the fact that Holland was now under Nazi rule. Our lives as Dutch Jews began to change drastically. Within a short time, new laws and regulations were in place in Holland. Jews were no longer allowed to live in the Hague and other coastal areas; universities with too many

Jewish sympathizers were closed. By the end of 1940 all Jewish civil servants had been dismissed and all Jews were forbidden to enter coffee shops and restaurants. Moreover, registration of the whole population had become mandatory. Doctors received new instructions for their medical practices, lawyers had their laws changed, and teachers were instructed to change history for the pupils by glorifying the German past. And who could have imagined that just over a year later Jews would have a "J" stamped on their ID cards and would have to wear a yellow star on all their street clothes?

With the German takeover of Holland, Nathan, my Jewish fugitive and father of Elly, was in serious danger. He tried to stay out of sight, but just after Elly was born in September the Gestapo found out where he was staying. Nathan was arrested and transported back to Germany. The family from whom he was renting said that one day he was just not there anymore. That was it. He was gone. I suppose it must have been known that he had fled Germany, and perhaps someone revealed his whereabouts. At first he was taken to prison; later I'm sure he ended up in a concentration camp. At first I received a few messages and information about him, but soon all this stopped. He did leave a letter behind indicating that he was Elly's father. With this letter, we could have claimed a good portion of money from Germany as compensation. Elly could have been the only inheritor of his estate, or what was left of it. Since she never knew her biological father, I would have liked her to have that at least. But somehow the letter was lost and we never were able to claim anything.

So there I was in Amsterdam without Nathan, looking after Elly alone. Feeling overwhelmed, I struggled through what seemed to be intensely difficult circumstances. Since I couldn't stay with my family I went to a special home for new mothers. Amsterdam had homes where new mothers could stay so that they could get on their feet again. It did not cost the mothers or their families anything. The city paid for it. Girls could stay for three or four months until things settled down. The home where I stayed had been a large private house. It now sheltered about twelve to fourteen girls all living together. There were four mothers and their babies to each bedroom. We spent most of our time looking after our babies, but we also helped in the kitchen and had light tasks to do around the house. After my parents recovered from their shock that I was an unwed mother, they came to visit me regularly at the girls' home.

During the time I had been seeing Nathan, I wrote to his mother several times. I knew her because she had come over the border to see Nathan now and then. After I had Elly, I wrote to give her the news. Although she wasn't very happy about it at first, I later received a letter from her indicating that while she didn't agree with our actions she had come to accept the situation. Like Nathan, she also disappeared. Perhaps she was sent to a camp as well. I wrote to her a few times but the letters were later returned to me unopened. Now I'm happy that at least she had one grandchild.

Because I had a child I was not allowed to return to the private Jewish hospital in which I had been training. I wanted to stay in nursing, but I couldn't while attempting to care for an infant at the same time. So my mother and my sister Jo took Elly in and looked after her. Because they were all living together in Amersfoort, they were able to do so. It wasn't too hard for me to let Elly go because she went to my family. To be honest with you, I had no idea what to do with a child. Since my family was nearby, I could visit Elly often. Every second weekend, if I could, I went to where my sisters were living in Amersfoort to see her and play with her.

Since I wasn't able to continue my schooling, I tried to find a job in my field. I managed to get a job in a Jewish rest home for the aged, which was also in Amsterdam. They took me because I had about a year of nurse's training already. Unlike in the Jewish hospital, I did not have to live in a nurse's residence, so I lived with a good friend from the hospital where I had previously trained. She was still living with her parents near the old-age home, and her father and mother let me rent a little room with them. Between work and visiting my family, I somehow managed to balance on the edge of stability, at least for the moment.

CHAPTER 4

Apeldoorn to Amersfoort

1941. More Jewish Laws. In the springtime, when the tulips were sprouting and the weather was growing warmer, the world was slowly closing off to us. Little by little, Jews were forbidden to enter playgrounds, parks, theatres, pools, libraries and hotels. We were being cut off from the world slowly, one prohibition at a time. With Bram seriously injured in the hospital, my father attempting to scrape together some business in Leeuwarden, Jo, her children, my daughter Elly and my mother crowded into my sister Henny's home in Amersfoort, our family was teetering on the edge. One day my father relayed some distressing news from Leeuwarden about our close friends, the Speyer family. They lived about two streets away from the house where I had grown up. Izaäk Speijer and his wife had three children, one daughter and two sons. I was friends with their daughter. To reach the core of the city they would have to pass our home, so they often came to visit. Izaäk was a merchant who had a cart filled with rolls of cloth for men's suits. He went to each home trying to interest the man of the house in buying a piece of cloth. The buyer would then need a tailor to make a suit out of the piece of material. This was how my parents had come to know the Speijers, especially Izaäk, and became friends with them. As a child I really loved licorice, and Izaäk would often stop by our home just to bring me a small piece. He would always joke that a fisherman from Urk, a fishing area close to Amsterdam, had found the licorice. He called it Urk-licorice. I remember really liking him.

My father told us that Izaäk's oldest son, Elkan, went out one night with some Dutch friends. Maybe they were being a little rowdy or tried to pester the Nazis. Who knows? But one of them threw down a sign in the park that said "No Jews Allowed" — as a joke. The same night the Nazis turned up at Elkan's house to arrest him. Not that he did the act. But because he was the only Jew in the group, the Nazis blamed him for it. Elkan must have realized that it wouldn't be smart to go home right away, so he wasn't there when the Nazis showed up. The Nazis waited and waited but then they lost patience and took Izaäk over to the police station instead. The next day the father was shot for the presumed "crime" of the son. We were horrified. Izaäk Speijer shot for no reason? And in Leeuwarden? It was impossible.

Later, after the war, I met Elkan Speijer in Montreal. He was married and had a child. He said that the rest of his family had been picked up and imprisoned while he had stayed out of sight until after the war was over. The regret was obvious. You could see it on his face, the regret that he was still alive when the rest had disappeared because of him. But how could he have known that a silly joke would have such a result? And would he have been able to save his family otherwise?

If the message was not clear before, it certainly was now. It was not safe to be a Jew. But somehow we still convinced ourselves that it couldn't get worse, that life was still bearable, that our fate would not be the same as Izaäk's. And for a while, it seemed as though we were right. I spent the year working at the Jewish home for the aged. I didn't particularly enjoy it, but I was glad I had a job, especially when I considered that Jewish life as we had known it was crumbling all around me. But by the end of 1941 circumstances were growing pretty grim in the Jewish hospitals in Amsterdam. Some of the non-Jewish doctors felt threatened by the Nazi regime because their laws, such as those requiring euthanasia, breached the Hippocratic Oath. Jewish doctors had it even worse. They could not obtain the equipment they needed and could work only certain hours because of the evening curfews set for Jews. Moreover, the Dutch weren't coming to the Jewish hospitals anymore because they were afraid to do so. The home for the aged where I was working wasn't as directly affected, but it would only be a matter of time before it would be.

The Nazi laws invading our personal freedom were also coming to seem even more oppressive. Not being able to sit in a café or the park and not being allowed outside whenever I wanted began to stifle me. And it was becoming more and more unsafe for Jews to be in a big city like Amsterdam. The Nazi soldiers made their initial invasion in Amsterdam and set up their headquarters in this city. More Nazi soldiers were stationed there than in the smaller municipalities. Moreover, we often could not discern who was a Nazi supporter and who wasn't. Since the Dutch N.S.B. did not wear a Nazi uniform, only civilian clothes, we had to watch every move we made around anybody, just in case the person was part of the N.S.B. and we upset them by what we did or said, or how we walked or looked. It was all secret. They could beat you up in the streets, and sometimes they quietly did away with people. They could kill you and nobody would give a damn.

Early in 1942 I heard that a small Jewish mental hospital in Apeldoorn had some open positions. I wrote them a letter to ask for the right to transfer and was accepted. Safety was becoming crucial and this hospital appeared relatively safe, partly because some of the doctors and many of the patients in this hospital were not Jewish, but largely because the German fist did not strike as hard in the smaller communities, at least not at first. I was motivated by more than safety though. I wanted to stay close to my family. Apeldoorn was a small city quite close to Amersfoort, the city where my family was staying. It was only about forty kilometres away, about the same distance that Amsterdam was from Amersfoort. I would still be able to visit them regularly. I also wanted to try to get my nurse's diploma, which I could not do while working at the old-age home. Since I had already done a year of schooling in the private hospital in Amsterdam, I hoped to continue my training at the mental hospital — not to be a registered nurse. That was impossible. But to gain some limited nursing credentials. And, of course, the medical staff in Apeldoorn didn't know me. Having a baby outside of marriage had damaged my reputation. I didn't want to stay in a place where everyone knew that I had had a child without a husband. I wanted to hide that part of my past and start over where people didn't know about it and wouldn't look down on me.

The mental hospital was located a couple of miles outside the city of Apeldoorn. The grounds had many trees and a beautiful garden. The hospital was not a single big building, but an assembly of buildings which dealt with different kinds of mental treatments. Each patient's history and illness was different from the next one. Men and women were housed separately in different pavilions. There was a building for the senile, or what might be classified as Alzheimer patients today. Then there was a building for the psychopathic, and another one for troubled teens who were on the verge of becoming criminals. A particularly large building was used to care for seriously mentally and physically disabled children.

Being in a new place, making new friends with the staff, and getting to know the patients, I felt that my life was beginning to look much brighter. I liked working with the mentally ill patients. Many of them were very sweet. Unlike in a normal hospital, where people constantly come and go, here the patients stayed for a long time, if not for life. So the contact between nurses, doctors and patients was close. We lived together like a family. My biggest joy was when I was sent to the children's building to help out. There, we would push the children in their wheelchairs through the beautiful garden with its different flowers and shrubs, and benches for you to stop and relax. Special teachers came in daily to educate the children as much as possible, so they could learn to do simple things, and perhaps even survive in the real world. Many of these poor kids were there because their parents could not or did not want to look after them. So we nurses, doctors and teachers became their parents and caretakers. They loved us and we loved them.

Not all the patients were loving, though. There was one female patient who was always angry. She would hit people and shout at the other patients and the medical staff. When she was uncontrollable she received a cold bath. After the bathtub was filled with ice-cold water, one of the staff members would undress her, sit her in the water, and then hold her face under the water for a short time. That was supposed to stop her violent behaviour, maybe cool down her hot temper or something like that. If that didn't help, we had a medicinal drink that would make the patient vomit. It is difficult to tell if such actions were for the sake of punishment or to cure the patient. In hindsight they seem unhelpful and even unnecessarily cruel. Such treatments are certainly not used anymore.

In fact, there is no comparison between medical treatments of that time and now. In the 1940's antibiotics had not yet been discovered. Seemingly small infections could not be held in check and often resulted in death. One of my friends, a male nurse working with me in the mental hospital, died because a patient bit him on the arm and the bite became infected. At the time you could only treat the infection with a poultice and hope for the best. In his case, the infection spread and we were not able to save his life.

In addition to the woman who was always angry, I also remember distinctly a man who would constantly recite the same thing: "When wagons were wagons and the ladies were easy, then we had a good time." It was a saying that rhymed in Dutch. One day when I was working near him and he came to the part, "and the ladies were easy," he crawled out of bed and came after me. When he reached me, he kicked me in the leg, knocking me down. When I couldn't get up a doctor had to come. I remember the man standing over me and laughing. Such escapades make my job sound frightening, but it wasn't. As nurses, we were never alone. We always had two people working together. Moreover, all the doors to the patients' rooms were locked and we had a wristband with all the keys. But there was never a dull moment!

One of our main goals was to help the patients manage their mental health problems and restore them as responsible members of society. There were rooms where patients could learn carpentry or shoe-making, the idea being that when they came out of the hospital they would have a profession. With supervision, the teens went to school in the village and some even received their high school diplomas. All the while, they would continue to be given treatment for anger management and behavioural changes. Often they went home after several years, and became responsible citizens. Since many of the younger patients were Jewish, they were also instructed in the teachings of the Torah. Lessons were held in the *shul* (synagogue) once a week in town and those of any age who wanted to come, and were physically able to do so, were welcomed. Of course, a fair number of people, especially the elderly, were not able to get out of bed, and so the Rabbi would come to visit them throughout the week.

The staff had close relationships not only with the patients, but also with each other. In the warmer months we girls would go up on one of the pavilion roofs and sunbathe, enjoying each other's company. Since we worked together and shared the same living quarters, we came to know each other quite well. We had a few music groups and often performed for the patients. Dr. Spanjard, a very talented man both in medicine and in music, led the groups. Our group performed classical music: Dr. Spanjard played the piano, I played the violin, and there was also a cellist and a flutist. We really enjoyed ourselves and the patients loved it.

During my days off, I would take the train to Amersfoort to visit my family and my daughter Elly. As I mentioned, my sister Jo and her children were living together with my other sister Henny and her family. My mother had lived for awhile in Amersfoort with Henny too, but because my father was lonely by himself in Leeuwarden, my mother moved back with him. My father was still trying to get a little bit of work — just enough to make some money for groceries and a little bit towards paying rent. But by 1942 he was making almost nothing. Most of their money came from a Jewish community fund. The community pooled their resources to give the poorer Jews some money so that they could live. My parents had to survive on that.

On one of the occasions when I came to Amersfoort for a few days, a young man stopped by Henny's house to deliver some meat. He was a Jewish fellow named Ernst Bollegraaf. The few Jewish people in the city got their meat from him. Meat was very scarce at the time. Each person could buy only 200 grams of meat every fourteen days, and to buy it you needed food stamps. Moreover, the Jewish people knew that the meat sold in the regular butcher shop had not been slaughtered according to Jewish rituals, and those who were very religious would not buy this meat. Understanding the problem, Ernst began doing some butchering, Jewish style, to provide meat for the Jewish community.

When he arrived with his delivery on this particular day, Henny invited Ernst into the house and he chatted with us. I learned that during the day Ernst worked together with his father in a recycling business. They had a warehouse where they collected used material, scrap metals mainly. They would assemble the materials and send them to another factory where the metals would be pressed together into big blocks and shipped to factories where it would be reused to make other things. At night when no one was at the warehouse, Ernst would arrange for a farmer to bring in a cow or calf and he would slaughter it there in the corner. Apparently, he had learned the butchering trade as an apprentice when he was still a boy. Sometimes peddlers in the recycling business would bring calves or chickens to the warehouse, which were hidden under the bales of clothing and rags they were delivering. Ernst would also slaughter these animals. And then, because he knew that all the Jewish people were hungry — all the people were for that matter, but he was concerned about the Jewish people — he would take choice pieces of meat and bring them around to the different homes. He would be paid for the meat, but not very much. Basically just enough to cover the cost of the animal.

Ernst was good looking and seemed to be a very pleasant young man. I thought he was nice but didn't take much notice of him. He noticed me, though. The same night he asked Arnold, Henny's husband, about me. "Is she free?" he asked. "I'd like to meet her again." Arnold replied, "Yah, she's free. But you should know that she already has a daughter from a previous relationship." Arnold told him my story and it seemed that Ernst didn't care. It did not discourage him from wanting to get to know me better. So I met him again and we began to spend more time together. I started to like him, and the more I got to know him, the more I liked him. He had a good mind for business but was also kind and generous. He was much closer to my age than Nathan had been, only three years older. And he was witty, charming and affectionate. We would go biking together for picnics on my days off. He loved me to death and swept me off my feet! It was hard to believe that he had fallen in love with me at first sight. He even wanted to marry me and be a father to Elly.

In June 1942, just a few months later, we were engaged. When I told my nursing friends of our engagement they were surprised and maybe even a little jealous. Apparently, Ernst was a real ladies' man and well known in the Amersfoort area. The girls all liked him because he was funny and flirtatious. But now he only had eyes for me. We planned to be married in October of the same year.

In the meantime I visited my in-laws-to-be, but did not come to know Ernst's family very well. The few times that I met them I liked them, however. My mother-in-law was a German Jewish lady and I remember that she was a terrific cook. His father was polite but he had a stern face, not at all like the friendly disposition of my own father. When I got to know Ernst's family, his sister Ilse, her husband, and their two children were all living in the house together with them. Ilse's husband, Herman, had lost his business; he had owned a butcher shop. So he was now working with Ernst and his father in their recycling business. It was clear to me that there was a lot of tension in the house and some competition between Ernst and his brother-in-law, Herman. Ernst was officially a partner with his father in his recycling business and was paid more than Herman. Between family dynamics, struggles for control and money issues, their relationship was strained.

I learned that Ernst had not had a very pleasant youth. He had been born and raised in Bunde, a small German town, home to his mother and her family. His father was of Dutch nationality but his mother was German and wished to stay close to her family after she was married. Ernst's father started a recycling business in Bunde, becoming relatively prosperous shipping the recycled materials out to different factories in both Germany and Holland. The company demanded long hours of work, and Ernst's father was seldom home to spend time with his son. The family had a permanent maid in the house, whose duties included raising Ernst and his sister Ilse. Apparently Mrs. Bollegraaf often suffered from headaches and nervous tension and did not have the necessary patience needed for dealing with her children. Especially for Ernst who was quite a handful as a young boy. When Ernst was a teenager, he had an apprenticeship in the butcher business. His father signed a contract with a butcher-teacher for Ernst to stay with him for three years. This butcher was a hard man. Each morning, Ernst was awakened by the noise of a heavy boot hitting the bedroom door. And if he did not get up immediately, he would receive a bucket of cold water in the face. While he did learn the butchering trade, those years were not happy ones.

It was only in 1938, after *Kristallnacht*, that Ernst's family moved to Amersfoort, so when I met him Ernst had not spent nearly as much time living in Holland as he had in Germany. They had to leave Germany because they were considered Dutch, even though Ernst's mother was German born. Ernst's father was Dutch, so that meant they were Dutch. But it wasn't too difficult a move. Since they had a sister business in Holland, his father was constantly back and forth over the border anyway. They had been living in Amersfoort five years when I met him.

It should have been a happy time for Ernst and me, preparing for our wedding. But that summer, the summer of 1942, tragedy struck us directly. As the Jews of Leeuwarden were systematically deported, my family was torn apart. By that time my father wasn't working at all anymore and my parents had moved in with a Jewish lady they knew, in the upstairs portion of the house. One by one, extended family members and lifelong friends were told to pack their bags. They were sent to Westerbork, the holding camp in northern Holland.

Westerbork was put into commission very early on in the war. It was initially built by the Dutch government to accommodate the thousands of Jews who left Germany and Poland, prior to 1940. Then when Germany invaded Holland, Westerbork was put to more sinister use by the Nazis — to serve as a holding camp for Jews prior to being sent to concentration camps in Germany and Poland. But nothing of this new development was known or understood, and even as they were being deported, the Jews of Leeuwarden tried to remain hopeful and feigned optimism despite their wariness. "Maybe we'll see each other again," they would say. "Maybe in Poland we'll have more opportunities and more freedom than we do here." Some had even chosen to go there already in 1940 and 1941, when Jews had been asked to go to Poland of their own free will. Many people did it. My brother Simon's sister-in-law, Clara, chose to go to Poland early on. There must have been promises or bribery involved that would convince her to go. Or maybe she thought that if she went, she could somehow save the rest of her family. I don't know. All I know is that she never came back.

Perhaps because my parents had moved from their registered

address to live with the Jewish woman they were initially overlooked by the Nazis. But when the N.S.B. came for the lady from whom they were renting, she called upstairs, "Mr. and Mrs. Dwinger, I'm leaving now." So then the Nazis knew that there were other people in the house. Otherwise they probably wouldn't have known that my parents were there because they had not been registered as living there; they were only renters at this time and not home owners. The Nazis quickly collected my parents, and along with the lady who owned the house, they were immediately transported to Westerbork, where they were kept for a couple of weeks. During that time, my mother and father wrote and told us how they had been taken and how, once they had arrived, they had been separated because men and women were housed in separate barracks. They didn't sound overly anxious or upset in their letters, at least not from what I remember. But perhaps they were just trying to protect us from knowing the seriousness of the situation. We sent them some packages with special food items, such as bread, cookies, candy, and hoped that they would return home. But they didn't. We never learned exactly when they were transported from Westerbork to Poland. We only knew they had left Holland when a parcel was returned.

My brother Simon had a similar fate. He and his family were living in Hilversum near Amsterdam. As I mentioned earlier, they had moved there quite some time before the war so he could travel more easily for his work in the photography industry. Initially he was summoned to move to Amsterdam with his family to live in the Jewish ghetto. But from there they were transported to Westerbork, and from Westerbork they were transported to Poland. What was happening in Poland was not at all clear to the Dutch population. We expected that our family was alive and would return after the terrible war was over. But my mother, father, brother and his family all ended up in Auschwitz. They never returned.

Ernst's parents were also deported around the same time: first to the Jewish ghetto in Amsterdam, then to Westerbork, and then we can only assume that they ended up in a concentration camp as well. The metal recycling business was of importance to Nazi Germany, so the Bollegraafs were initially free from deportation. Certain professions exempted Jews from having to go right away: jobs that were useful in the war movement, such as those connected with recycling and other technical trades, as well as anything connected with medicine. The Nazis, however, must have reasoned that they didn't need two Jews to run the recycling business. One Jew in charge was plenty. There were fewer and fewer reasons to keep Jews around, and more excuses to deport them. I never really knew my husband's parents.

October eighth was our wedding. But there wasn't much to celebrate. Both our parents had already been deported. My brother and his family were gone. I didn't have a wedding dress. No wedding party. I borrowed a pretty navy-blue dress from a friend of mine — also a girl who never came back — and we went to the town hall for our marriage. The religious ceremony had to wait until after the war; it was not advisable in case the Nazis thought we were mocking them, and we certainly did not want trouble. It was a very small wedding, only a few family members — those who were left. It was small enough to fit into Henny's dining room for dinner. After we came back from the war, we had our religious wedding. I didn't have a wedding dress for that one either. I have no pictures from either occasion. With the war raging on, and in the midst of Jewish persecution, weddings, dresses, parties and pictures did not seem very important.

After the ceremony, life went on as normal, if it could be called "normal." Our sense of "normal" had been radically unsettled with the deportation of our parents, but we tried to find stability beyond the tragedies of the present and insecurity of the future by carrying on in ways that we recognized as having been stable and secure in the past. Since life did not halt, we had to move with it. I went back to work in the hospital in Apeldoorn and my husband Ernst lived in his parent's house with Ilse, Herman, and their children. We visited each other on my days off. Or rather, I came to Amersfoort to visit him. My husband refused to come to the mental hospital. I would invite him to visit me but he wouldn't come. He told me that because my room was upstairs in one of the female pavilions, he'd have to pass by the women patients on the lower floor. Most of the women were sexually charged and were obvious about wanting him. The one time he came they actually tried to cling to him. Since the male and female patients were housed separately, it was a big deal to them when a man, outside the regular hospital staff, was in the hallway. It made him very uncomfortable.

As I mentioned, Ernst and his sister and family were temporarily free of deportation because of their recycling business, but things weren't going well. To help with things, Ilse decided to assist her husband and Ernst in the warehouse by packing recycled material like clothes, copper, paper, glass and even rabbit skins that were to be pressed into blocks. The smaller the parcels, the cheaper the transport to the factories. They also had some clandestine help: some non-Jews who had long been employed in their business. But these workers could not be seen. Jews were not allowed to employ non-Jews as workers, and the Dutch non-Jews were forbidden to work for Jews. If the non-Jewish Dutch workers heard an unfamiliar noise outside the building they would dive into a box of clothing, often dirty, smelly, and full of lice. Finally, the Nazi police came and investigated. They had probably been told that there were "non-Jewish" employees in the warehouse. They did not find anything, but when our workers came out of hiding, they were so frightened they were blue in the face and hardly breathing. After that, we stopped having Dutch people help us.

The next three months were relatively calm considering the chaos going on around us. Then early one morning in January 1943 a phone call from my husband roused me out of my bed in the nurses' wing of the hospital. He was part of the Jewish board of directors in Amersfoort and had received notice through them that in the next couple of days, German soldiers and officials had been ordered to take over the mental hospital. As I listened to him on the phone, it was clear he was really anxious and upset. In a very few words he warned me of the danger: "You have to get out because the Nazis are coming!" He ordered me to come home immediately. Without delay I alerted the hospital administration office, but they had apparently already been forewarned. Immediately discussions began about what to do with the patients.

A few hours later, while we were trying to decide on a course of action, a train arrived full of young Jewish men. They were prisoners from Westerbork who had been sent by the Nazis to help in transporting the patients. To where? To some great camp they kept telling us, where they would be very safe. We didn't know exactly where they meant, nor were they particularly clear. They had been told that if they did not do what the Nazis wanted, their own families, who were still in Westerbork, would surely be killed. Later we learned that these young men, who had been in Westerbork for at least six months, had been sent out many other times to do this type of dirty work for the Nazis, always under threat of losing their families should they not comply. They were friendly and we could see that they were happy to be out of the camp for a few days themselves. They spoke highly of their treatment at the camp and told us not to worry — that if we went, the food would be good and we would be treated very well. But we had our doubts. The night they stayed at the hospital, we slept on the floor while they took our beds.

Very early the next morning, there was a frantic knock at one of the nurse's doors. Susan, a friend and fellow nurse, was summoned; her husband was on the phone. He needed to talk to her immediately, which was unusual as it was still dark out. Susan grabbed me and wrapped her arms around me. We knew the news would not be good. By the time she reached the phone there were a number of people up already, clustered around. Her husband told her exactly what Ernst had told me the day before. In fact, several warnings had arrived, all with essentially the same information as mine: the hospital was about to be taken over.

At this point, the board of directors, administrators and doctors decided there was no time to lose, that they must release the patients who were able and willing to be released. This was not an easy decision, since there were patients who would be a danger to themselves and others. Quickly we helped patients into their clothes, made sandwiches for them to take along, and gave them money for train fare and lodging. We tried to be as calm as possible so as not to upset them, all the while urging them to go. We could do no more for them. We knew that in Germany mentally handicapped patients were being killed. So what was to become of our patients left nothing to the imagination.

I stayed a couple of hours to help, but I knew that the Nazis would be arriving soon and that I needed to get out, as Ernst had warned me to do. After doing all I could, I went to my room. What to take with me? My eyes swept over the room. Clothes, letters, photos, other valuables? I took almost nothing, just what would fit into a little handbag. I had to leave my beautiful Italian violin behind, the one my brother had bought from an old violin maker. It nearly broke my heart to do so. But when you are so close to disaster, such things do not seem to matter. The only thing that was important was my life. I saw personal possessions as things that I could retrieve or replace when this nightmare was over.

I dressed in simple street clothes, took off my Jewish star, put some money in my pocket, and left my identification behind. Before I left I asked several doctors and nurses to go with me because Ernst's house was large enough to accommodate them also. If I could save myself, maybe other people could be saved too. I told them, "Look, we are in danger if we stay here. I'm going away. I have to go home." There was a brief pause. "You can't just go," they replied. "We have to stay with the patients." The medical staff didn't think the Nazis would do anything to them, the patients maybe, but not them. I shook my head. "No. I'm leaving. If you want to come with me, come with me." But nobody wanted to leave the poor patients. It was especially difficult to leave because the friends and staff members became really angry at me for going. They looked at me as a traitor; they were so dedicated to their work that they were angry about my departure. I probably would have stayed too if my husband hadn't been so adamant on the phone that I come home. I knew I had to look after myself first. It had really come to that point.

Looking as innocent and as confident as possible, I headed towards the train station in Apeldoorn. I made an effort to stroll down the country road, and once in the town I tried to create the impression of a casual shopper by looking nonchalantly into the store windows until I reached my final destination, the train station. All I could think was, I have to get to the train. I have to get to the train. On my way there, I met and saw many of our patients whom we had just released. For years, they had been very dependent on the staff and when they saw me, they wanted to talk and go with me. To them I was a nice nurse whom they knew very well; they wanted to grab me by the arm and go with me. But I acted as though I didn't see them. I whispered, "Go away." Or I ignored them. I was unwilling and afraid to acknowledge them. I heard later that many of them had been picked up by the police and soldiers because of their frightened behaviour and outbursts. Some of them in fact ran all the way back to the hospital. They just couldn't handle being free and having to look after themselves in all the panic and confusion.

Angelina, a girl in her early twenties whom my husband had known in better times, was one of them. She had become ill with manic depression a few years earlier, and had been staying at the mental hospital. Because she was not dangerous, she was one of the ones we let go when we tried to empty out the hospital. But she went back; she didn't know what to do outside the structure of the hospital.

I felt ashamed when I met the patients on the streets and they wanted to come with me. Often when I think about it now, I feel terrible and ask myself whether it was wrong of me to ignore them. Couldn't I have saved some of them too? But how could I have taken them with me? Somehow I got to the station, bought my ticket, and boarded the train. Apeldoorn to Amersfoort was less than an hour's train ride. But it seemed to take days. I was sick with nervous tension. I felt awful. Numb. It seemed to take all the courage that I had just to sit there. I found a newspaper and attempted to focus my attention on it. I tried to give the appearance of reading but I just stared through the words. I could hardly read the headlines with so much going on in my head. No one greeted me at the other end of the train ride. I went through the city, again looking into store windows, trying to stroll inconspicuously, as people do. But let me tell you that I was extremely happy and relieved when I reached my house and the front door closed behind me.

Was I a deserter? This question pops up in my mind even now. About an hour after my departure, the army trucks loaded with soldiers rolled into the hospital grounds. In a flash, the pavilions were surrounded and emptied out. The patients were loaded into those ugly trucks and everything was left behind, even their personal belongings. But this procedure did not go smoothly. Some of the patients went berserk. And when they would not, or could not cooperate, they were severely kicked and beaten and forced into the trucks. There were even patients, bedridden or hardly able to walk, who were shoved into the trucks. Lastly, the patients in straightjackets, shirts that bound the patient's arms to his or her body, went also.

It seems that the same happened during the train loading. Even the nurses and doctors who were appointed to take care of this poor assemblage of people could not calm them down. Regular medicine, even if it had been brought along, could not be given because the patients had no water and would not swallow the pills. It was a horrible predicament. The patients were ordered into the baggage wagons that were waiting for them. There were pushed and bludgeoned to move faster, wedged body-beside-body into those windowless wagons. The big sliding door finished the job. No air could circulate, and the patients went mad: people could hear them screaming, having seizures, wildly hitting the walls, and attacking each other in a total frenzy.

I'm not sure what happened to them from there. Some people

said that the doctors and nurses were told that they had to accompany the patients to their destination, that there would be work for them in Poland and Germany to further their profession. They also said that the train never went farther than just over the border into Germany, where deadly gasses were pumped into the wagon, killing everybody. Others said that only the patients were gassed right away on the train but that the medical staff were taken to Auschwitz. There were still others who said that patients, doctors and nurses were taken first to Westerbork and then all sent to Auschwitz. In some ways it doesn't make much difference. They ended up being gassed, whatever way you look at it. I lost so many good friends then.

While I am writing this manuscript, I have tears in my eyes when I think about this experience. How could it be that in one day the whole hospital was emptied of patients, doctors, nurses and many more professional employees? I was so lucky to have escaped. The Jewish doctors, nurses and other personnel who did not go with this transport were brought to Westerbork, registered, and after a few days were transported to the death camps in Poland and Germany. Only a few came back after the war. Most perished in those camps.

Rhodea at age sixteen.

An early National Socialist Movement (NSB) parade on the canal
street in front of Rhodea's home in Leeuwarden.

Rhodea as a young girl (centre) skating in Leeuwarden.

Rhodea as a young woman working in an office.

Rhodea's husband Ernst Bollegraaf, at approximately age nineteen.

The Apeldoorn psychiatric hospital in which Rhodea worked as a
nurse in 1942, and from which she fled to go into hiding.

Rhodea and Ernst at their engagement party, June 1942.

Rhodea's photograph of Ernst while on a bicycle ride
in the country soon after their engagement.

"The Star of David patches, that were sewn to our clothes."
"Jood" is Dutch for Jew.

Deportation of Dutch Jews to Westerbork transit camp, c. 1942. Courtesy of the United States Holocaust Memorial Museum, Lydia Chagall.

Dutch Jews on route to Westerbork transit camp. Courtesy of the United States Holocaust Memorial Museum, Trudy Gidan.

CHAPTER 5

In Hiding

I was home now and thankful to have escaped the terror that awaited my colleagues. But what to do next? Had they reported my departure? Did the Nazis check the personnel list? Was I still in danger? Would they come after me? Whatever the answers, one thing was certain: my husband and I were at the end of our semi-conventional lives and were now forced into making a new one. But we did not know yet how.

Staying alive was all that counted. Money, education and the other things that seemed of utmost importance before meant nothing to us anymore. The time would come, as we later discovered, when nobody would be free in Holland to live their live they had known it. There were the ever-more severe punish and degradation of the Dutch population. The Nazi dominated the bigger cities and many of the Dutch ci not necessarily agreeing with Nazi ideology, wanted to stay on good terms with them. On the one hand, they were not pro-Nazi, but on the other hand they were not pro-Jewish either. In the cities, the anti-Jewish sentiments were stronger because Jews were often regarded as taking business from their Dutch counterparts. However, in the *Achterhoek*, the backlands of Holland, many people in the farming communities were violently opposed to the German tyranny. They opened their doors for the unfortunates, a group to which we now belonged. At this point, though, we were totally unaware of the Underground working in the rural areas of Holland and how they could help us.

Initially we took what turned out to be a futile and almost fatal road. After talking over our options for a day or so and trying to figure out a solution, we decided to go into hiding in Amersfoort. Ernst did not actually need to hide at that time because he was still authorized to work in his business. But we reasoned that since I had disappeared from work, Ernst would have to disappear too. I knew it wouldn't take long before someone realized that I was missing. Eventually the Nazis would come looking for me and find Ernst. Ernst talked about the predicament to his tennis partner, Mr. Venema, who was his good friend. For years they had been playing together in a tennis club. Mr. Venema and his wife offered us the upstairs of their house. It was in a secluded area near the edge of Amersfoort, and we were so thankful to them. We took the next few days to put everything in order. Mr. and Mrs. Boer, who lived across the street from Ernst, and various other neighbours were already storing some of his parents' things from the time the Bollegraafs were deported. Mrs. Boer agreed to take in more items, so we left some furniture with her: a beautiful desk, an old wall clock, and the bedding, if I remember correctly. I put all the linens and blankets in a big tea crate and sent it over. They were beautifully embroidered for my mother-in-law and worth quite a lot, not just in monetary terms but also in personal meaning and family history. In Germany, where my mother-in-law grew up, brides-to-be received all their linens as gifts and they were personally embroidered with their initials. Since we had no linens of our own, we had been using their personalized ones.

My husband ordered a large amount of groceries to be delivered to the Venema household, hoping they would last us for some time. He had collected food stamps and bought a lot of food "under the table." Because of his butcher business on the side, he had many connections and was able to buy extra without the stamps. Then we took out all the money we had stashed away in case of an emergency. Most of the Bollegraaf business money had already been given to the family who owned the grocery store where my mother-in-law had always done her shopping. They were kind people and had offered to hide money for Ernst's parents. They had taken a tile out of the kitchen behind the stove and put the Bollegraafs' money, along with their gold and silver, in a small hole behind it. Then the tile was put in place again. We gave our personal money to the Venemas to hide. We trusted them so much that we handed over a large roll of bills, which they put into a secret spot, behind a wall in one of the rooms.

Before we left, Ernst talked to Herman, his brother-in-law, and tried to convince him to lock up the house and business and have his family go with us into hiding. We were sure we had enough money and food for all of us, but they did not want to go. Perhaps it was because of the strained relationship between them, or they felt that their own safety was not yet in jeopardy. Or perhaps Herman believed that if he stayed he could become the boss and inherit the business. Whatever the reason, they did not accompany us. Late the next night, we took some clothes and other necessities we thought we would need during the first week or month. We had no idea at that time how long our stay would really be. The Venemas seemed eager to help; we thought that they really liked us and wanted us to be in their home. How wrong we were.

We stayed with them only one night. The next morning when we woke up and our friends had gone to their jobs, we found a note shoved under our door. It said that we were not safe with them, the police knew where we were, and that if we did not want to be caught, we should leave at once. So there we were, with just the clothes we wore, out on the street, afraid that around every corner there would be a policeman, or worse, a Nazi to arrest us. On the very streets that we had walked the previous week with some sense of security, we now darted along furtively. We were devastated. We had already experienced many disappointments in the past two years, but we did not expect to be out on the street one day after we had gone into hiding.

Ernst decided that we should walk to the edge of Amersfoort where he had another friend, a farmer, whom he knew well. My husband had always gone to their farm when he was selling meat. Now, he reasoned, the farmer would be kind enough to take us in. How did we do it? What kept us going? I do not remember. But we reached the outskirts of the city, breathing a little easier when we saw their farm in the distance. We hoped fervently that they could do something for us. And they did. Once Ernst explained our situation, they agreed to hide us in the attic of their barn. Sleeping on straw was not particularly comfortable, but at least we were safer here than on the streets. They invited us into the kitchen to take our meals with the family. We had to be on the lookout constantly, however, peeking out the window to see if anyone was coming. If the police had decided to do a house search, they would have found us immediately. Luckily, no one came. We were grateful to this farm couple for hiding us for a few weeks. They really wanted to help and they did not ask for any money. Thank heavens, because even if we had wanted to pay them, we had nothing left to pay them with. When we tried to retrieve some of our money that we had at the Venemas for safekeeping by sending someone who was sympathetic to our predicament to their house in order to collect our clothes and money, the Venemas refused to give us anything. We now realized that they were not sincerely our friends but interested only in our savings.

Ernst and I had no idea how difficult those first few weeks would be. We had no money or clothes to speak of. We were wholly reliant on the goodwill of the farmer who hid us. Every day we hoped the war would end. How long could this war possibly last? But with the German occupation we did not know. To make matters worse, we received some terrible news while we were in hiding. The farmer returned one day to tell us that Herman, Ernst's brother-in-law, had been ordered to report to the Amersfoort police station. A policeman whom we all knew, and who was not a member of the N.S.B. party, had come to the Bollegraaf house with the message for Herman. Instead of going together, as if Herman were being arrested, the policeman told Herman under his breath to "go now" to the station, saying, "I will come later." He thought Herman would understand his coded message: to "go now" meant to get out of there and go into hiding. An hour later when this police-man came to the station he was shocked to find Herman there waiting for him. There was nothing that he could do for Herman at that point and Herman was arrested.

That left Ernst's sister, Ilse, alone with her two children. Ernst sent her a message, inviting her, begging her, to join us at the farm. The farmer would come after dark and pick the family up at the back door. This was very risky for the farmer but he agreed to take the chance. Unexpectedly, she replied that she did not wish to join us and that she would rather be with her husband. She surely did not think of the children, those innocent little souls. A week or so later all four disappeared and we never saw them again. We still do not know what happened to them.

While we were reeling from this news, a letter was delivered to the farm written in the same handwriting and style as the first one the Venemas had slipped under our door. It said basically the same thing, that we should leave. The Venemas must have written it as well. Apparently they knew where we were hiding and, likely because they had our money, wanted to make sure we were far away. We knew that we were unsafe, that too many people knew where we were, and that we were putting the farmer and his fam-ily in serious danger.

But we didn't know what to do. We knew we had to leave with-out delay. But to where? The only place we could think of was my sister's house. Perhaps we could stay with them while we figured out what to do next. My two sisters and their families were still living together in Amersfoort, but I did not want to bring any trouble upon them by going to their home. At the moment they were still free from deportation. Bram had received an exemption letter from the German leader in Holland indicating that because he had been seriously injured during the war, he and his family would be protected. As long as he was in the hospital for treatment, they would not be called up for transportation to a concentration camp. For this reason we continued to have Elly stay with Jo; she was safer there than with us. However, despite the fact that Bram had been suffering in the hospital since his almost fatal injuries in 1940, we all knew that this promise would not last forever. It was only a matter of time before they would also be deported. During this time, Jo received a small monthly allowance, but not enough to survive on. They were barely making it. When we could think of nothing else, we reluctantly went to Jo and Henny, who took us in even though they could not support us and knew it was dangerous. But we knew we couldn't stay. Their house was right in the core of the city. And to our regret, we could not now help with expenses, and food stamps were scarce. How could you feed two more people on food stamps which were already not enough?

But help came again. In the hospital in Utrecht, Bram had met some influential people who belonged to the Resistance movement, or *De Ondergrond* in Dutch. In this group was the husband of Holland's Princess, Juliana — Prince Bernhard. When Prince Bernhard married Juliana, we thought, Oh no, a German Prince, but although he was German by birth and even an officer in the SS Corps in the early 1930s, he showed himself to be pro-Jewish after marrying Princess Juliana. When Queen Wilhelmina and the royal family left Holland to seek refuge in England, Prince Bernhard did whatever he could to improve the plight of the population, and particularly the Jews, by helping to form the Underground. At the hospital, Bram became friends with other soldiers who had connections with England and were part of the Underground. Together they made sure that he stayed in hospital as long as possible. There was also a woman, a volunteer who came to the hospital to visit the patients periodically. She was in the Resistance too. Through the soldiers and this woman, my brother-in-law learned about the Underground and became involved. As it turned out, they were busily engaged in finding a hiding place for Jo and the children, as well as Henny, her husband, their family and my daughter Elly. They were also working on finding families who would hide other fugitives.

In a few hours, contacts were made with the Resistance, and a few days later we received the message to be ready very early in the morning with our suitcases packed. They had found us a family. The next day we left, five minutes apart, carrying a small suitcase each and trying to look as confident and inconspicuous as possible. Ernst had a woman with him and I had a man with me, strangers to whom we pretended to be married. Together with our companions, we boarded the train in different compartments, not revealing that we knew each other, so that if things went wrong only one of us would be arrested. We brought no identification, which would have been punishable if we were asked for it. Such a trip was a big risk. If we were caught we would be deported right away, and so would our helpers. But we were desperate. We took our chances because we knew that at this point there was no other way.

The train took us to Winterswijk, less than an hour's journey from Amersfoort. Here we had to transfer to another train. This one took us to Varsseveld, our destination. Varsseveld was a small town, not much more than a few houses, in the Achterhoek, not far from the German border. We were told exactly what we should do when we reached our destination. Again we were to go our separate ways and meet a few streets from the train station where we would find a cart or hay wagon, something like that. There would be a person to meet us who would accompany us to our place of hiding. I don't remember what was going through my mind during that journey. I know we were on edge, and by the journey's end all I could focus on was getting into that wagon as quickly as possible. We were fortunate that no one caught us. Everything went just as planned and we arrived safely. We were lucky. Many people who did the same were not nearly so lucky.

A pleasant family, the Ankersmits, greeted us in our new home and showed us our hiding place, which was where we were to reside for the next months or maybe years. Nobody could tell how long it would be. The Ankersmits, who lived on a small farm, gave us a place to stay in one of their barns. In Holland, the barn was most often attached to the back of the house and was used to house the farm animals. A door would take you straight from inside the house to inside the barn. The barn would also have a side entrance from which to take out the cow manure. The manure sat just outside the barn in a big pile waiting to be used as fertilizer for the next year's crop. The Ankersmits had a small barn, with only ten or twelve cows, since they did both dairy and vegetable farming. At first we thought that this cow barn was to be our new home. Thankfully, our abode was located in another barn about one hundred meters from the house, in what had once been a pig sty. The pig sty was a little room no bigger than ten feet by ten feet with a small semi-circular window. The eating trough had been removed. In the corner was a bed made of straw, some blankets and pillows, a very small table, two wooden chairs, some shelves for our belongings, a couple of pails of water and an old carbide lamp. The barn was not very warm when we arrived in the winter of 1942, but it did keep out most of the wind. We had no complaints.

Mr. and Mrs. Ankersmit were in their forties and had two children, a son and daughter in their late teens or early twenties. They were a religious Protestant family and treated us very kindly. Most days we would eat with them in the kitchen. They fed us well. I particularly remember breakfast. They made their own bread, so we had tasty white bread in the morning, which was considered better than dark rye or whole wheat bread at the time. We would also have a nice boiled egg and bacon. We ate better than we had in Amersfoort.

Early in the morning at around six a.m. Ernst would help with the milking. Then he had to bring the pails of milk to the road. At eight o'clock the milk would be picked up by a truck from the milk factory where they produced pasteurized milk, butter and cheese. The farm was far enough away from the town that he could do so without worrying too much about his personal safety. My husband was also fortunate in that he didn't look overly Jewish. He could pass as a farm hand. I helped with the housework: dusting, sweeping, cleaning the kitchen and doing the dishes. When I was finished I would go back to our room in the barn and rest. Luckily, I was able to do some knitting and sewing as well as darning the family's socks to keep myself occupied.

In hiding, we had only a few pieces of clothing with us. From the Underground we received a couple of pants, shirts and a sweater. I wore dresses. When it was colder, I would wear shorts under my clothes, which functioned as warm underpants. We had to make do with very little. I remember owning a brown wool fishbone patterned coat. Since we had no heat in our room, I wore this coat every day to keep myself warm. Of course it became shabby in a few months, but instead of throwing it out I loosened the side seams and turned the coat inside out. I then sewed the pieces together and closed up the front. Now I could wear the coat as a dress. I wore this dress for a few months until the sleeves became thin and frizzy. Since the dress did not look particularly attractive any more, I took my scissors and cut out the tattered frizzy pieces of the sleeves and lowered the neck somewhat. Now the dress was transformed into a warm undergarment. Again I could wear it for a while. But nothing lasts for ever. New holes appeared under the arms and the lower part became very thin. I looked at the mess, and again snipped out a few pieces. With those pieces I could make a warm pair of underpants. I am sure you will laugh when I tell you that when they became thin, together with the cut off pieces, I sewed two warm bags for my hot water bottles, and even then the leftover pieces did a service. After the war when we could set up a household again, I made two or three thick pot holders that I used for many years. When I finally had to get rid of them because my fingers went through the holes and were burned by the hot pots, I felt as though I had lost a good friend.

Living in a barn, as you can imagine, we had little available in the way of sanitation. In the morning my husband went in to the house for a kettle of hot water that the Ankersmits would leave standing on the stove for us, as well as a little wash basin. They had a water pump inside the house. He would bring out the warm water and the small amount that fit into a kettle would have to suffice to wash the both of us. We didn't wash our whole bodies. Just our faces, arms, and under our arms. I don't remember ever taking an actual bath while I was there. We were as clean as possible, considering the circumstances. You could do a great deal with a little bit of water. Our toilet was in the animal barn attached to the house. It was a wooden board with a round hole in it and a pail underneath, similar to the one we had in Leeuwarden when I was a child. But if we had to go to the bathroom at night, we would usually just go outside. The room itself was not the cleanest, but I don't think we noticed that much. I would sweep it up and tried to keep it as neat as possible.

And we had some uninvited guests: mice that brightened our lives. Especially at night, by the light of our lamp, they would run up and down the rafters and steal our food. Now I shudder when I see a mouse, but then we did not fear these little furry creatures. We feared only people. The mice were so common that we even encouraged them by putting some corn on a chair beside our bed and watching them come as close as they dared to steal the kernels away. It was times like these, the jokes and the laughter we shared, that helped Ernst and I to survive our time in hiding. Despite the difficulties and hazards of our situation, our lives were never in such danger or so appalling that we had to despair. We lived for the moment because that is all we had for certain. And in the moment, if we had food and a place to lay our heads, then that was all we really needed or wanted. We had no money, no future and no past. We stopped thinking of what had happened in earlier years, and we didn't try to plan where we were going. It was a strange moment-by-moment existence that allowed for pleasure within a world of difficulty and danger.

Since the Nazis focused first on attacking and cleansing the bigger cities of Jews and other undesirables, many people hid in the smaller farming communities rather than in the big cities. As I mentioned earlier, there were also more anti-Nazi sentiments in the farming areas and kind people were more able to help because they had the food resources on their farms. A farmer always has more survival resources than people in the urban centers, so our adopted farm family was able to make life as comfortable as possible for us. They were more willing to help as well, because it was not as dangerous to hide people in the countryside. Nonetheless, they were at risk, and the punishment was severe for hiding people. The punishment would be the same for them as it was for us. We would all be deported. Consequently, we did all we could not to expose ourselves or make any noise.

Often, probably about monthly, we would receive a coded message from someone in the village advising us to hide ourselves. There tended to be (and needed to be) a lot of co-operation among the citizens of the smaller towns when farmers in the area had people in hiding. It was easy to recognize if someone in the community was hiding people — it was difficult to keep it from the rest of a small community. So communities would work together. If someone in the town knew that the police or Nazis were up to something or on the prowl, they would send a coded message to the people who were hiding Jews or others against the regime. The code was something like, "Uncle John is coming" or "Aunt Betty is coming." Then you knew you had to disappear. The Nazis would periodically do house searches at random. When they left the office or station, no one would know for sure where they were headed or which farm they might be checking. But thanks to the codes, at least we knew when they were out and about.

Some farmers had double walls in their homes, or in the corner of a room. They would sometimes have a cabinet, and behind the cabinet was a wall with a hidden entrance. It would be just big enough to fit two or three people standing up. Such people would sometimes have to stand up for the whole night. The first time we had to hide at the Ankersmits, we were hidden in a small space in the wall. We had to go up into the attic where there was a trap door that opened into the wall. There were a couple of chairs in the space behind the wall, one behind the other, just like in a show. But it was no show let me tell you, sitting there in the dark. The space was not deep; it had just enough room to sit. We used this hiding place only once.

Soon after the Ankersmits had taken us in, they also took in a wealthy older Jewish couple, maybe in their fifties, who did not have any children and who could pay the Ankersmits for hiding them. I'm sure they were paying more than the Underground was paying to look after us. They lived in the house with the Ankersmits, rooming in a small pantry on the main floor. When there was a coded call, they would use the hiding spot in the wall.

If there was word of a general danger in the neighbourhood, we would hide in our room in the barn for a couple of days. Late at night on these days, our food would be brought to us. When we received a more urgent coded message, we hid outside, usually in a deep ditch under a little bridge, until the coast was clear. There was also a wooded area behind the property so we could hide between the trees as well. It was actually much safer than hiding in the house or the barn because the Nazi police tended to search the houses and barns thoroughly for hidden Jews, while the grounds and land around the farms were not carefully combed.

Oddly enough, I don't really remember being afraid in these moments of hiding. Maybe we had lost all our fear. When we were wholly focused on trying to save our lives, we had no fear anymore. Fear tends to be an anxiety about what may happen or what could happen. But we had no future; we lived for the moment. Saving our lives seemed to move us beyond fear. It was more about action than fear: get out, save your life, do what you have to do.

Through all of this, we were always grateful for the care and love our new "family" showed us. Even today, I am very thankful and every night before I go to sleep, I pray for all the helpful people who saved us through this ordeal. Whether they are living now or deceased, I will never forget them. How they could do this, I couldn't tell, for we were not the only fugitives they had to care for. We never came to know many of the Resistance workers. We only knew that there were a lot of God-loving people who worked for the well-being of all the people in hiding, be they Jews or non-Jews, and whatever their professions, from manual labourers to doctors and lawyers. Indeed, many of the non-Jewish fugitives were in hiding because they could not in good conscience agree with the new laws or regulations ordered by the Nazi regime, all of which were designed to erode the Dutch democratic spirit in favour of German totalitarian ideas.

* * *

Very soon after we went into hiding, my sisters Jo and Henny also went into hiding. I believe Henny and her family went into hiding first, leaving the house to Jo for a short time. It was April 1943 when Jo was sent her "relocation" instructions, that is the letter from the Nazi office telling her to pack a small suitcase for each member of her family, after which they would be taken in a few days to Vught, another of the Dutch concentration camps. She obediently followed the order. At the same time, however, she contacted Jan Kanis, the Underground leader in Amersfoort. Mr. Kanis set the wheels in motion to provide a vehicle that would pick up Jo, Bram and the two boys on the evening before their "relocation." Bram, I have mentioned, was still more or less an invalid in the hospital at this time. On the day of the family's planned escape he managed to have himself sent home — with the help of a bribe. Once the family was together and prepared, they waited behind closed curtains all night for the truck that was to take them to safety. It never appeared . In the meantime, a Mr. Hagenau from Utrecht, a man who worked with Jan Kanis in the

Underground, came to take Elly away to his home in Utrecht for a few days until another place could be found for her.

Early the next morning, after they had almost given up all hope, they learned that the truck had broken down. A new plan was hurriedly put in place, and a car suddenly appeared to collect the family, and through a pre-arranged signal, their escape began. The two boys were sent out the front door, and when they had walked a little ways down the street into the next block, Jo appeared at the door with Bram on his crutches, and they left the house together. They closed the door behind them as if they were going on a simple errand, and stepped into the waiting car. The car then drove slowly down the street to where the boys were walking, stopped to pick them up, and continued on through the city to a "safe house" run by the Underground. It belonged to a Mr. Van Der Weij and his two adult daughters, Bep and Ina. All three members of this brave and kind family were teachers; they took enormous risks to help escaping Jews. Our family owes them a great deal, for they saved Jo, Bram and the boys from almost certain death.

Jo's carefully packed suitcases, which had been placed at the back door for later pick up, were never collected because the truck that had broken down the night before had so delayed their escape that there was no time to do so. In fact, when Jo and her family did not show up at the train station that morning, the Nazi officials dispatched soldiers to their house to see why. When they broke in the front door, they discovered the empty house and the suitcases at the back door. Seeing no one in the house, they took the suitcases. For the rest of the war Jo, Bram and the boys spent most of their time hiding at different farms near the town of Alderbruck. Through it all, they managed to stay together as a family.

All except Elly. Elly did not hide with Jo's family. If she had stayed with Jo and Bram, she would have had to stay inside for several years. Moreover, at this period, Elly was only three and young enough to unwittingly be a danger to the rest of the family. Shortly before their escape, Jo asked the Underground to find Elly a safe hiding place in the country. A Mr. Hagenau from Utrecht, a man who worked with Jan Kanis in the Underground, came to take Elly away to his home in Utrecht for a few days and then arranged for her to live with a family with children in the south of Holland. The Underground reasoned that amongst the other children in the family she would have more freedom to play outside without causing a great deal of suspicion. And if anyone suspected that she did not belong to the family or was not a visiting relative, they trusted that the small town was sufficiently closely knit that no one would tell.

Neither Jo nor Henny ever talked much about their experiences in hiding, particularly not the bad ones. They both focus on the good aspects of hiding, grateful that their lives were saved. But I do know that when they first went into hiding they hid together in a tiny basement that was actually underground. It was not easy, because apparently Henny's husband, Arnold, was difficult to be around, especially in such close quarters. Before the war he had been a business entrepreneur and a coordinator in the circus industry, and he was the kind of person who wanted to have things "just so." Earlier he had insisted on boiling water on Henny's little stove to wash his socks every day. Now in hiding, he still wanted to have his socks washed every morning even though there was no water in their underground quarters. He also wanted to have certain things to eat that were just not available anymore. He couldn't stand the narrow quarters. He was the sort of person who did not adapt well to the new and not exactly pleasant circumstances and he drove the others almost crazy. Not too long after, they moved away and hid with another farmer a little farther away. Besides the odd story here and there, I never learned much besides the fact that they were all right and managed to survive the war.

We had been at the Ankersmits a couple of months and were finally beginning to adjust to our new life in hiding when, without wanting it, I became pregnant. Certainly it would have been better had it not happened. In fact, in our circumstances it almost seemed like a terrible crime for me to become pregnant. We knew that a baby would not be a welcome addition to the family because it brought a much higher chance of discovery and a much greater risk to our host family. If anyone heard the baby cry, we, the Ankersmits, and the other Jewish couple staying with them, would be done for. We tried to think of ways to undo the pregnancy. Ernst was convinced that it would help if I ate soap. I have no idea how he came up with this crazy notion, but somehow he reasoned that with soap we could get rid of the baby. I was ready to try anything. The soap we had available to us at the time was a soft soap we called green soap. You took a cup to the grocery store and they had a big barrel of it there with a scoop for you to buy by the pound. It didn't come in bars, nor was it the consistency of dish detergent. It was more like glycerine soap. It tasted terrible. Somehow I managed to swallow it, but after a moment it all came back up again. And of course I was still pregnant.

We knew we had to tell the Ankersmits. After we revealed to them what was going to happen, their attitude changed towards us like the colour of a leaf in the fall. While they didn't say or do anything purposefully nasty, they stopped being friendly. What could we do? The fact was there. And this sudden rejection by the kindly Ankersmits hurt us deeply, even as we realized that they had to be concerned about their own safety.

After I became pregnant we were also not fed in the same way we had been before. We did not receive as much to eat and were always hungry. We were also often given our meals in the barn now rather than being invited to join the others in the house. While the older Jewish couple were cared for hand and foot, and received white bread, bacon, and eggs in the morning, we were given some heavy dark rye bread with a slice of cheese. Moreover, I suddenly wasn't needed to help in the house anymore. The older Jewish woman now helped the farmer's wife with the household chores, and I had only that cold old shed in which to amuse myself. My husband was still working and milking the cows, but he never had enough food to satisfy his hunger. Often in the morning before he brought the milk to the road after the cows were milked, he would lean over the full cans and drink up the cream that had settled on the top until he was satisfied. I'll bet you that the milk had very little cream in it after he was finished.

In the past we had often been allowed to join the others in the kitchen for a bedtime snack, and this custom the Ankersmits sometimes continued, but now we were always so ravenous that we tried to eat as much as possible. The common Dutch bedtime snack was a kind of porridge with lots of milk. It was very tasty, but there was never enough to satisfy our hunger. We knew that outside the backdoor in the corner of the barn the Ankersmits generally kept a number of big baskets piled with apples and carrots for the winter. I recall how on the way out of the house after the snack my husband would making walking noises, as if both of us were walking out to our room in the barn, while I stopped to pick up a couple of apples and carrots for us. Thankfully they never noticed us. We didn't want them to know that we were stealing extra food after all they had done for us.

I must say that it did not surprise us that the Ankersmits were upset with us when we told them I was pregnant. We were worried too. A baby was dangerous and could unwittingly betray all of us with its crying. The punishment for being discovered was surely death, for the fugitive as well for the hosts, either in a concentration camp or on the spot. It had already happened in the neighbourhood. We had heard about two elderly sisters in our village, retired schoolteachers, who were also hiding Jews — sometimes as many as eight at a time with ages ranging from university students to elderly couples. But eight mouths were too many to fill. In a house where two people lived before and where all of sudden there were ten, life became very difficult. Everybody in the community loved those old ladies, and every local family had at least one or two children whom they had taught, at one time or another. So when our host family and many other farm families who were hiding fugitives gathered their harvest, some of this food, along with milk and meat, was secretly delivered to the old ladies' house. This was all very hush-hush, but you never know how some talk gets around. And nobody really knows why, but in the middle of the night, suddenly the old ladies and their "guests" were all awoken by a pounding on doors and windows by the SS, kicking and shouting like madmen. Right away, everyone in the house was chased into a waiting vehicle. Later on we heard they were all shot.

Both the host families and fugitives tended to be on edge, well aware of the danger they were bringing to themselves and to others by hiding. In fact, there was a situation where an older Jew was shot by the Underground from fear of his risking the lives of others. When I think about it now, I presume that he was suffering from some kind of mental or emotional disability, because he was constantly angry and confused and often threatened that he would not stay in hiding, that he would shoot any German who came near him. One day he slipped out of hiding and began walking on the road to the village, cursing loudly. The farmer had to hurry out and bring him back to the house. The situation became worse and worse — especially because the farmer had other people with children in hiding as well. So the farmer asked for help from the Resistance. The old man might well have been quite respectable before, but too many lives were at stake because of his erratic and dangerous behaviour. The Resistance sent a few men to check on the situation. When they realized how confused this man was and the serious danger he was putting himself and everyone around him in, they decided that there was no other option but to do away with him. This was not an easy choice for the people, but what could be done? This man would be a menace to anybody in any hiding place. But still, it was a terrible thing to have happen.

Our only contact with the outside world was through one of the men who belonged to the Resistance and who had accompanied us to the farm. Early on, he provided us with fake identity papers from Dutch citizens who had died. Our identification papers said that we were from Delft. My name was Nelly. I don't remember what my last name was. But in hiding, everyone called me Nelly. My husband also had another name. It was one way to try to keep the police from suspecting that we were Jewish. If they caught us, they caught us. The papers wouldn't make much of a difference. But at least we had something to show if we were travelling and asked for our identification papers. It made us feel more secure.

Every member of the Resistance had certain duties and obligations to fulfill. Our contact was in charge of getting additional food stamps for the fugitives in hiding. Along with other members of the Resistance, he would steal extra stamps from the safes where they were waiting to be distributed to the non-Jewish population on the first of each month. You could not get much food for these stamps because food items were sparse in the stores. Nonetheless, for many city dwellers the stamps were a matter of life and death. With the food they obtained, they were able to keep from starving. And for the farmers, the stamps brought in an extra supply of food with which to feed hiding fugitives.

When our contact found out I was pregnant, he brought us, beside the food stamps, diapers, wool, needles and whatever else he could pick up for the care of the expected baby. Every time he came, it was like a little sunshine in our drab existence. He even had, at times, some letters from my sisters who were of course also in hiding, and I always had some letters ready for him to take to them in return. Writing letters and knitting for the baby at least gave me something to do during those long hours sitting alone in the barn. Every time he came, he told us about the progress of the Allied forces, which always lifted our spirits. He gave us strength and courage to endure this terrible time in our lives.

We saw that this man was too busy to visit all the fugitives on the dozens of farms, so my husband offered to assist him, and thus he became helpful to the Resistance movement. Soon, more and more fugitives were added. Before long my husband was well-known among the farmers and well-acquainted with the neighbourhood and the small, hidden country lanes through the cornfields. He offered to distribute the food stamps to farmers who were hiding people. When the moon was out, he could find these farmers easily late at night, riding on an old bicycle. I didn't have a problem with him doing it; I thought it good that he wanted to help the Resistance that had been so helpful to us. Although he was a strong man, he took a gun with him for extra security on his nightly rounds. Ernst knew how to use a gun, since he had received training when he had been in the Dutch army during the short war between Holland and Germany in 1940, but I don't recall him ever having to use one while we were in hiding. Many a night when I was going to bed, he followed his secret path to deliver the food stamps and other messages to those people and friends of ours. It seemed relatively safe, or maybe I just chose to think it was safe in order that I wouldn't worry about him.

Once during his nightly travels, my husband had an interesting experience. He was riding his bike to bring food stamps to the Jews and other fugitives in his neighbourhood. It was a moonlit night and while pedalling down the country road, he could see the path without his flashlight. He knew the road well, so he didn't really need much light, and of course the less light the better, for his own safety. Suddenly something startled him: two dark figures darted from the road into a ditch on the side. They were apparently not German soldiers, since they would have confronted him rather than jumping from the road. Leaping off his bike, he used his flashlight to examine the ditch. He probably thought the dark figures were Jewish fugitives. But to his surprise, the two men were wearing army uniforms. They acted scared and held onto each other. Their faces were white and frightened; they surely thought that this was going to be the last minutes of their lives. My husband could have shot them and probably would have done so, if he had thought for one second that they were Nazis or collaborators. But with such frightened faces, he knew right away that these people needed help. Quietly he worked to calm the men down. But not understanding him, they came out of the ditch with their hands up to surrender. Since my husband was on his route to the next farm, a short distance away, he motioned the men to follow him. Now he was not only bringing food stamps, but as a bonus, two men.

The two men, however, were an unwelcome gift for the farmer, who already had three or four Jews in the house, and did not want to care for two more people. The men told the family that they were Russian soldiers who had been imprisoned by the Germans after they had conquered their battalion, but that they had escaped before they were locked up. The farm family wanted to help, but they could not really take care of them. The house was full. Still, far out in the field there was a small empty chicken house where they could stay. So every night my husband brought leftover food and coffee from the dinner table to them. This went on through summer and fall, but once the snows of winter arrived, the imprints of his wooden shoes became visible from the road to the chicken house. Another solution had to be found.

Fortunately my husband was a good negotiator and was able to find them a place with another farm family in their attic. Here they stayed for more than a year, until the war ended. Afterwards they went home to their own families in Russia. Later on they wrote the farmer's family and thanked them sincerely. They were happy to be home again. They wrote a couple of more times, but then it stopped. Life goes on. And in Russia, which suffered so much loss of life, everybody had to find a new place in society and the communist regime needed every able hand to reconstruct the country.

Ernst also helped the Underground collect coal and peat for the surrounding Dutch families. A railroad track ran close to the farm we lived on, which was about ten miles or so from the German border. Most of the coal meant for the Dutch to cook and keep their houses heated was sent to Germany. The railway company specialized in the transport of wagonloads of all kinds of merchandise and articles for the Nazis as well as for upper-class German society. Twice weekly around eleven o'clock at night, a train would pass with one or two wagons full of coal, to be used for heating in Germany. It did not matter that the Dutch families were shivering in their houses and apartments; nothing seemed to matter to the SS, who left us no coal, no food, no money, no jobs.

The engineers on the trains were Dutchmen, who were usually forced to do this dirty job of stealing from the Dutch and transporting all the goods to Germany. Despite the Nazi regulations, however, some brave railroad workers would roll big blocks of coal and sacks of peat off the train when it neared the farm so that it could be collected and distributed to the farmers in that vicinity. A whistle blowing in the distance was the signal. My husband and the son of one of the nearby farmers would wait by the tracks with a wheelbarrow each, as huge chunks of coal were thrown or rolled off the train. In the dark, they took the wheelbarrows and ran towards the tracks to collect the coal, peat and other materials that could be burnt in the kitchen stove. As a result, two or three wheelbarrows of coal went to the different surrounding farms so that every housewife could prepare and cook a meal for their extended families, and the farmhouse and hiding places could be warm and cozy during the night. Along with supplying the area with coal and food stamps, the Resistance helped provide hundreds of other important items for fugitives, items such as medicine, vitamins and newspapers printed in English that told us about the war's progress. Newspapers printed in Holland were censored, so without the Underground we were left in the dark about the political situation.

Then one day a terrible thing happened. As I have already mentioned, our contact from the Underground would visit us every month. But one month he did not show up. Instead, a week or so later another gentleman showed up with the stamps and letters and two blankets for the baby. With great anguish, he told us that our contact, his colleague, had been caught, imprisoned and probably already shot by the SS. Along with some others, he had broken into a building to steal food stamps, but somebody had discovered their actions and squealed to the authorities. The SS were hiding in the building. When the members of the Resistance opened the door, the Nazis were waiting for them. All were arrested, handcuffed and taken to an unknown place. We were shocked by what he told us, for our contact had been so good to us, and we loved him for his ideals and his unselfishness. We prayed and hoped against all odds that our first contact (we never knew his name) would be safe and come back after the war. Later we heard that he had not even been transported to a concentration camp, but that shortly after his arrest he was shot to death along with the others. We never forgot him and in our minds we know he died a hero's death, caring for and loving his country and the people he helped. After the war, the Dutch government and the Queen's family commemorated the citizens who gave their lives for Holland. The families left behind were honoured with a sum of money so they would not suffer. But of course those families would much rather have had their loved ones alive and in their presence.

Life goes on, heedless of our sorrow, and Ernst began to help this new contact, distributing food stamps as he had done before. Thankfully, this contact stayed with us until the end of the war. As for us, it now seems strange that throughout our ordeal, we never gave up hope; we were optimistic that we would somehow survive. Sometimes in the night, when the English airplanes were going overhead we would sneak outside and sit in the field to watch them on their way to Berlin. We prayed to God to help everybody who suffered there. Some nights when we sat there, we could also see the northern lights. Somehow the beauty of these white or pale blue shifting lights far away encouraged us. Compared to that of so many other people in the city, in the jails and concentration camps, life was reasonably good for us. Even in my pregnant condition I trusted that God had a great gift for me, however difficult it would be to have a baby at this time. And even the unkindness of our hosts didn't really touch me that deeply. The biggest problem was the monotony.

When I speak of the people in the concentration camps, it should be remembered that, when we were in hiding, we did not know how terrible the camps were and that they almost always led to death. And maybe it was a good thing that we did not know that all our families who were imprisoned were already burned to ashes. If we had known I don't think we could have maintained our optimism about the future and about our families' reunions. We may have lost hope altogether. After the war, the knowledge of their fate hit us very hard. In fact, once we found out, it was harder in some ways than the long years of being in hiding.

What I really regret is that I didn't convince my parents to go into hiding with us. Why couldn't we do that? When we went into hiding, they could have gone into hiding too. But then again, I'm not sure that they would have. They were not young anymore, and at the time many people thought that going to Poland wasn't such a bad idea. I just wish that we could have saved them. I miss them terribly. I can never think about the war except in terms of the family and friends I lost. Even now, the knowledge that all our loved ones, friends, families and everyone who suffered in concentration camps and jails did not survive their ordeal makes me jump out of bed in the middle of the night with tears running down my cheeks. Although it was sixty years ago that all this happened, even now it is unclear to me why the Jews were so hated and even nowadays continue to be persecuted in certain groups. It causes me to try to be benevolent and understanding, and to avoid confrontation or judgment of others who are different from me. This is the only light that I see now.

When my pregnancy became more visible, my life became more isolated and dreary. I did not go into the house anymore at all. Not being able to do any work in the house, and not really being allowed to go outside for the sake of our safety, there was nothing for me to do during my pregnancy except sit shivering in my little pigsty. I spent most of my time writing letters to Jo and Henny and knitting a lot of baby clothes, usually in pink or blue. We did not know if our baby would be a Johanna or a Johann. From all my knitting I had leftover blue and pink yarn that I used to darn Ernst's dark socks. They were quite a sight. Ernst owned only three pairs of wool socks during this time. Walking in wooden shoes is very hard on the socks, but you keep wearing the wooden shoes because they are warm and waterproof. Of course new holes appeared after a few weeks and so I darned on top of the repairs already done. Ernst grew at least an inch by having so much darning under his feet. It sounds terrible but at the time we laughed, hoping that this extreme thriftiness would not have to last forever. We looked forward to a time after the war when we would be together as a family and able to buy dozens of pairs of socks.

The laughter did me good because I was truly miserable during the last months of my pregnancy. Bored and despondent, I was sitting almost all the time, since I couldn't go out and exercise during the day. The way the baby was positioned gave me a sharp nagging pain in my abdomen. As my fingers were numb from the cold, knitting was no longer possible. I tried to read and even started reading the Bible that they had left for us. There were so few books. It helped to concentrate on something other than the dull pain. At night I was sometimes able to walk outside in the field, which helped a little. But we had to be careful that nobody saw us. I felt irritated and impatient. I just wanted the baby to come and the war to be over. Yet I knew that giving birth while in hiding would not be easy. To produce a new life in this hellish world made us realize that we were not solely living for ourselves any more. How could we feed the baby? How could we keep it warm in the middle of the winter? And what if the baby cried and passing people heard it? And what about the diapers? Where could we wash them? Lots of questions, but no answers.

My pains worried me, for I knew I hadn't had the exercise a pregnant woman needed. Then the baby stopped moving, perhaps from my own lack of movement. I was sure I should be seeing a doctor, but of course I couldn't. As the town doctor had promised to help when the baby arrived, the farmer and his wife were not too concerned, Actually, I suspected that they would have been pleased if we had just disappeared. I felt awful, like an outlaw. And the little bit of food I ate was no help. Thinking back now, I cannot blame my hosts. They did not ask for this kind of danger.

Our baby girl entered the world in a barn on the cold afternoon of December 6, 1943. When the pains started, the daughter of the family went to town to bring the doctor. However, the doctor could not be reached. He was not home just then and nobody knew where he had gone. I was frightened. It seemed that we were alone with this birth. Ernst had already put together the tools: rope, scissors, flashlight and a kettle with water. Very primitive and not very sterile, but this was all we had to work with. I needed someone who knew exactly what had to be done. Here we were blessed with another kind of miracle. The older Jewish lady who lived with the Ankersmits came to our aid. She told us that she had been a registered nurse before they went into hiding and had often assisted the doctor and knew exactly what to do, even in complicated cases like mine, where it appeared that the baby was lying feet first. In such cases the baby had to be turned around inside the mother in order to be able to get oxygen as soon as possible, so its brain would not suffer from lack of air.

There was pain. A lot of pain. And nothing could be done for it. But the nurse worked very professionally and quickly got the baby out and made sure that it could take its first breath. It was a girl! Her breathing went less than smoothly, and her skin was an unhealthy shade of blue. But thankfully she was breathing, although very shallowly. She was clearly cold and it did not help that our room in the barn was unheated, that the wind blew through the cracks in the wall.

Ernst was there when I gave birth. He stood at a distance watching. While the nurse was trying to help the baby breathe, it was my husband's job to cut the umbilical cord. Unlike the doctor, who knows exactly where to cut it, my husband tied a string around the umbilical cord right up against the baby's body and cut on the side of the string closer to the baby. He cut it so close that she ended up with a hole, a very deep navel. She had a navel but so deep down inside her body, you couldn't see it.

I kept the baby close to my body under the blankets, and later in the evening when my husband came to join us, she lay in between us. It was a wonder that we did not crush her. We watched and listened to her taking breaths, not regularly yet, but more regularly than before. Then we must have fallen asleep, for when we woke up next morning we saw a beautiful pink baby lying between us breathing regularly. She was so adorable, with plump rosy cheeks and fine blonde down growing on her little head. We could not believe it. We dark brown-haired people had a blonde child. If she had been born in a hospital we would have thought that someone had switched the baby. But there was no doubt she was ours. We had already picked out the name — Johanna — after my sister. Thankfully our fear about her crying was unfounded. Johanna never cried, not even at birth, probably because of lack of oxygen, and not after because I would feed her right away, and then she slept until the next feeding. It was almost as if she knew that she should not cry. So it went for about two months. But the fear that she would begin crying was always there in our minds, as I am sure it was in the Ankersmits'.

Despite her coldness towards us at this period, Mrs. Ankersmit did lend us an old-fashioned baby carriage along with blankets and accessories from her attic. With a warm water bottle, our little Johanna moved to the carriage. Soon after her birth, however, her skin became very red and her little bottom quite raw. This was probably because the soap I was using was too harsh, and the diapers could never be washed properly. We had only cold water, which made their drying impossible. In the barn there was a line, but in the morning when I needed those diapers, they were still wet, if not hanging frozen stiff. Don't forget, it was December. I had no powder or ointment. I tried to comfort Johanna by cleaning her little behind with my own spit, and it did help somewhat. After the baby was ready for the day, I found that all I wanted to do was to creep into bed again, where I lay with no ambition or desire to do anything. I was not allowed to come into the house with the baby, and being cooped up in the barn day after day, I found that unless my husband dragged me out of bed in the morning or I had to get up to attend to Johanna, I wouldn't budge. I just wanted to stay in bed all my life. Depression set back in.

Later we were allowed to hang the diapers over the stove in the kitchen during the night. But the next day, when they were dry, they were also dirty from people drying their soiled hands on them. This was done on purpose, we knew, by the farmer, who by now really did not want us there. Every day we felt more and more strongly that we couldn't stay. Finally at the beginning of February 1944, we asked our contact on his next visit to find us a place where we could feel welcome. After a few weeks we received the message to be ready on a certain day, late at night, when we would meet some people who would accompany us to our new hiding places. I say "hiding places" in the plural, because we could no longer be together. It was too dangerous to hide as a family with an infant. I knew I would be inconsolable if I had to give my baby up to strangers, but I also knew in my heart that it would be best for the child if we went our separate ways. The farewell to our farm family was also emotional. I knew that for them it had been trying, but we were alive and healthy, and it was all thanks to them. They had kept us safe, and to this day I am thankful to them for their protection.

CHAPTER 6

Buried and Concealed

W hen the moment to leave arrived, a few members of the
Resistance came to the Ankersmits' farm to take us our
separate ways. Parting from Ernst and Johanna was another one
of those moments where I didn't have time to think or grieve. It
just happened. It had to be done, so we did it. We did not want to
be separated but we had no choice. It was for the sake of our own
safety and for that of our new host families. Our emotions and de-
sires kept being sacrificed to safety; it was always our primary and
utmost concern. We just hoped it wouldn't be long before the war
was over, before we could see each other again and live together
in freedom. And then, as was believed, our families would return
and we would have an enormous reunion. The thought of their

homecoming and the anticipation of our own freedom kept me going. We had to survive.

I was not allowed to know where Ernst and Johanna were taken. Nor could they know where I was. It turned out that our different hiding places were only about ten miles apart, but at the time I had no idea of the whereabouts of my two-month-old baby or my husband. Again, this was for our safety. If the Nazis or N.S.B. police found one of us, we could not say where the others were because we honestly didn't know. If we did know, they would squeeze this information from us and we would endanger each other. We each went with a different member of the Underground. A lady came and took little Johanna, pretending the baby was her own so she could travel with it without raising suspicion. She would bring her to a wealthy farming family who had many children. Ernst was taken to a host family near the town of Geesteren, where he worked for a farmer who was also a horse breeder. I went to an old-fashioned farm near the village of Borculo, about five miles outside the town itself.

My new host family was a gracious and good-hearted couple with two children. In total, there were seven of us living together: the host couple, their two children, the husband's brother who worked with them on the farm, a grandfather who was likely the original owner of the farm, and me. The house was only one storey. It had three bedrooms and a big kitchen. I don't remember if they even had a living room. In the corner of the kitchen was an easy chair for grandpa. I was the only person hiding with this family and I was lucky to have my own bedroom inside the house. It was a small room, just big enough for a single bed and a little closet for clothes, but it was my own space within the family home. After living in the pigsty, it seemed like an incredible luxury. In one of the other bedrooms were two large beds for the parents and the children. In the other bedroom slept the grandfather and the husband's brother. The bathroom was located outside — a good old fashioned outhouse. They were not a particularly well-off farm family. Compared to the Ankersmits, they had a harder life, yet they were incredibly generous and gentle people, easier to get along with than our previous hosts. They never spoke unkindly to me. But then again, I also wasn't pregnant while I was staying with them.

My role in their home was housekeeping and acting as a nanny to the two children. I did the sewing, the cooking, the cleaning, the laundry and looked after the children while the rest of the family worked out in the fields. I made sure that when they came home there was food ready on the stove. We would fatten up and slaughter a pig now and then. As a kosher Jew I was not supposed to eat pork but I ate it anyway. I was not really practising my religion at that time, and what with the shortage of food I ate whatever I could get my hands on. I was not picky. They made a lot of their own *Wurst* (a kind of salami or sausage) and they would save the pig's blood in order to make *Bludwurst* from it. I don't eat the stuff anymore, but at the time I thought it was delicious. They had a few cows mainly for milking, a couple of chickens, and they planted corn and a few other vegetables. When cooking vegetables, I would use the entire plant. I cooked up the green tops of the carrots, with a little bit of butter, some salt and pepper. We also ate the tops of the beets. Early on in the war I had started using entire vegetables. Even before we went into hiding, the monthly food stamps did not provide enough to live on, so we'd have to salvage everything we could. With the stamps we couldn't buy much meat, and definitely no eggs. On the farms we had a much healthier eating situation than in the city.

While I didn't mind the work or the care-giving, I found it ironic that I, a mother of two children, one of whom was just two months old, was placed with a family who had a baby boy three months old and a young girl of about five. The members of the Resistance must have thought this would be a perfect place for me. But can you imagine how I felt, having to care for somebody else's children while my own Elly and Johanna were away from me?

Every time I looked at those children, sweet and good as they were, I could not help thinking of my own two girls. Where were they right now? What were they doing? How were they growing up? I felt desperately lonely. While I was hiding at this farm, I made Elly a rag doll and gave it to the Underground to send it to her. I learned after the war that the Underground had sent her to the village of Mechelen, in South Limburg, the southern-most province of Holland. It is located between Maastricht and Heerlen, and is north of the Belgian border. The province was freed in September 1944 by the Allies. But at the time I worried for her safety, hoping that she would find the doll a comfort and a play-mate. Sometimes it was hard for me to see how well the baby was treated: a warm bath in the morning, clean soft clothes and a snug little crib. By contrast, my own Johanna had been greeted in the morning with a little pan of lukewarm water and some frozen dia-pers with the dirty spot not washed out. I cried often thinking about this, and prayed and trusted that in her new home she would have the care she deserved.

The area of Holland where I was hiding was particularly unsafe in the winter of 1943 and the spring of 1944. I could not go out-side the house often since we never knew who would see me. If the wrong person found me, that would be it. The large anti-Jewish party in Holland would do anything to bring Jews to their death by reporting them to the German Nazi party. Although I was careful, I think that the neighbours must have been aware that I was hiding with this family. It was hard to keep them from knowing. Neighbours really had to trust each other in these small towns, as well as work together and help each other. Hiding fugi-tives became a real community effort. One of the neighbours was a woodcutter who worked together with the grandfather in the host family where I was staying, cutting down trees for firewood. They were close friends. This man knew for sure that I was there. Many of these Dutch citizens were happy to help each other out and support unfortunates like ourselves. But even so, we had to be careful; you never knew who might suddenly join the party ranks.

It certainly didn't put me at ease to know that the nearby village of Borculo housed a Nazi headquarters. If someone wanted to squeal, they didn't have far to go. But generally the community was on the alert; messages flew back and forth to and from the village and we often received warnings that the Nazis were on their favourite mission: house-searching. At regular intervals the Nazis went around to different farmhouses, a few a night, and carefully searched them. They did not often come in the daytime to look for Jews or other hidden fugitives. When we were warned about these searches, I had to go into a special hiding place outside. This place was a hole in the ground in a wooded area about a hundred meters behind the house. The hole was less than a meter deep and just wide enough to lie down without moving around. It was the shape of a grave. The host family had put some straw in the hole to keep the damp out as much as possible and create a makeshift bed. And I would take a cushion and blanket from my bed with me for extra padding and warmth.

After I climbed in the hole and made myself as comfortable as possible, lying on my back, the farmer would cover the hole with a board and camouflage it with moss, leaves and other ground-cover so no one would notice the hiding space if they were searching the woods. This hole was okay when it was summer and dry weather. Holland is a wet country, however, and I often came out of this hiding place dripping because of the rain seeping through. I had a lot of company in there: all kinds of bugs, spiders, worms and anything else living in the ground. At night these little visitors would crawl under my blankets. In the morning when I woke up, I found that I had squeezed some to death by rolling over on top of them. After the all-clear, my hosts would open the hole and I would crawl out and start my daily work. It wasn't the most pleasant of hiding places, but I actually slept quite well down there, and when it was dangerous I was grateful to have a safe place.

It may sound frightening and claustrophobic to be hiding under the ground, as if dead. But as I have mentioned, fear became secondary or even non-existent in those situations where my life was at stake. It was as if I lost my fear during the moments I was in the most danger. Was it partly because I didn't realize the seriousness of the danger that I would be in if I were found? Or was I so wholly focused on the moment and the need to hide, that I lost all anxiety and worry about what might happen? I could never figure it out.

I stayed with this host family for what I think was about six months, although it might have been longer. Looking back now, it's difficult to get the exact lengths of time straight. But eventually we decided that it was too dangerous to stay there. With the Nazi headquarters so close to us in Borculo, we were often on edge. Every day we saw them driving their big army trucks over the road not far from us. I asked our Underground contact about the possibility of moving closer to my husband if a host family in the near vicinity could be found. I missed him terribly. My contact agreed to search for a place closer to Ernst, and for some reason it did not seem so important now that we be kept in isolation from one another.

Finally the moment I was waiting for came: our connection approved my engagement as a housekeeper and nurse not far from Ernst. Only a couple of farms over. They moved me to Geesteren where Ernst was also living with a host family by the name of Kelholt. Now we could be together more often. We were both overjoyed at this change in my location. Nonetheless, my leaving a good family touched me deeply, and I promised to come and see them in Borculo when everything was over. And we did. As a matter of fact, we visited every family we stayed with as well as other people we knew from the war years a number of times.

In my new hiding place I lived together with an elderly man who had suffered a stroke. He was living alone and could not look after himself. Again I did housework and cooking. Because of my training as a nurse, I also looked after this old man, who had to be helped with everything, including feeding and going to the bathroom. He had one son who did well on the black market and paid me a few guilders for looking after his father. But I wasn't there more than two months when the elderly man began telling me that he was going to die. He passed away shortly after. Somehow he knew.

After the elderly man died, I was able to move in with my husband at the Kelholts' farm where he was working. We had already been spending some time together, as the farms were close together, so the Kelholts had come to know me a little and graciously agreed to take me in. I was thrilled finally to be able to live with Ernst again. It was now late 1944 and we had been living in separate places for almost a year. Ernst's hiding place was in the attic of the stable, separated from the rest of the barn by bales of hay. One of the large bales could be pulled out and that was the entrance to my husband's little room. Someone would have to move it in order to let him in or out. He had been in hiding by himself during that whole year.

He filled me in on some of the interesting occurrences that had happened to him in the meantime. The farm on which he was hiding had a lot of land and a big field of vegetables, so he was busy from early morning till late at night. There were many farmhands, and nobody suspected that he was a Jew. In the first place, he tried not to do less work than the others and having been on a farm before, he knew everything there was to know. In fact he was even quicker milking the cows than the others. And when the farmer saw that he knew how to handle horses, he was often given the job of leading the two workhorses to and from the field behind their house and feed them too. The farmer was so pleased that Ernst was good with the horses that he was asked to assist in the main business on the farm: breeding pure-bred horses.

On this farm were two stallions and six mares. Besides breeding their own horses, the Kelholt family allowed members of the farming community in the vicinity to come and have their mares bred. My husband was now in charge of this procedure. About August 1944, the Nazis needed horses. They normally acquired them by simply coming to the farms and confiscating them, promising that after they won the war, they would pay for them. I don't think any of the farmers believed this, but to be rid of the Nazis they gave up their horses, hoping that the soldiers would not come back. The less they saw of them the better they felt. One day, just at feeding time on the farm, some big trucks rolled in over the sandy road.

My husband saw them coming but he was not afraid. He already knew what they were coming for.

The Germans could be polite and sweet if they wanted something, and the farmer invited them in. At the same time, he gave Ernst a signal — "Fix them up." Understanding what the farmer meant, Ernst headed over to the stable. Speaking in German, the farmer said that he was happy to contribute some of the horses for the sake of the war. "*Danke*," said the Germans, bowing deeply to show their gratitude. By now it was summer and the mares were free in the fields while the two stallions were in their stalls. When the farmer brought the Germans out to the stable, my husband had busied himself feeding the stallions. They knew him so well that they would let him pet them all over. "*Ja, diese. Die sind aber schön*," said the Germans, seeing the beautiful horses and immediately wanting them. Sure, they could have them, said the farmer. At this point Ernst led the first stallion out. The horse walked calmly with Ernst as he always did, but when the German leader rushed over to take the reins, all at once the horse reared up on his hind legs, apparently ready to attack. Meanwhile the second one, still in the stall, was so aroused by this commotion that he tried to jump over the little dividing door. "*Nein, nein,*" shouted the Germans, jumping back and dashing out of the barn in terror. Once outside, they glanced nervously back at the horses. They promised to come back but never did.

Ernst also became more involved with the Resistance movement in Geesteren. On one occasion he went with another man to the village at night to help move a sheriff and his family out of their house. The sheriff had decided that he did not want to follow the Nazi laws and was planning to go into hiding with his family. That night, just when they were busy emptying out the house, a troop of Nazis came around the corner. Ernst and the other man who had come with him to help jumped behind a hedge. But already they had been spotted. The Nazis started shooting at them. They didn't get Ernst, but the other man was killed. It was such a close call.

Later, the Underground started to help out the stranded Allied troops. The Allies had invaded the coast of France in the summer of 1944. We were all so happy, and were expecting to be freed in a few weeks. The German army was said to be in chaos, and was retreating rapidly. It turned out, however, that we had got our hopes up too soon. "Operation Market Garden" — the plan to capture the bridges leading from the Netherlands into Germany as a means to push back the German army and drive into the heart of Germany's industrial centre in the Rhineland — failed. Among the Allied forces were British, Polish and Canadian boys who became trapped between two big wide rivers in the southern part of Holland: the Rhine and the Maas.

According to the broadcasts we were receiving on "Broadcast Orange," the Dutch Underground radio based in England, we learned that there was a mission to capture the bridges over the Rhine leading into Germany at Arnhem. One large group of American Allied paratroops crossed the bridge over the Maas close to the city of Nijmegen, but when the British Allied paratroops on the other side approached the other bridge by Arnhem, the Germans had that bridge so heavily guarded that it was impassable. They had thought the German defences in that area were poor, but in fact they were able to pin down the Allied troops in a fierce attack mainly from the air. At the same time, the Allies had already passed one bridge so they could not go backwards any more, and forwards was equally impossible. The German army was at their front and their rear now. This was a situation they could not get out of by themselves.

Moreover, the rest of the Allied forces had no chance to free their comrades and were just waiting in the vicinity for reinforcements. This of course takes time. Troops, equipment and weapons all have to be brought over, and in the meantime a large number of Allies were imprisoned in no-man's-land, as you might well call this slice of Holland. Those soldiers needed food, medicine and other necessities to survive until they could evacuate the area. My husband got on his bike and with a few other dedicated men rode to the river, just fifteen kilometres from his farm. There was a small boat waiting and all the collected food was loaded in. Silently, they rowed to the other side. The food was surely very welcome. This was dangerous work but personally rewarding for Ernst. In the end, we heard that just over 2,000 Allied troops were able to cross the river successfully at this time, with many others being killed or captured. We had thought that this attack on the German army would defeat them quickly. However, the sad truth was that the northern part of Holland was not actually freed until eight months later in May 1945.

Now that we were together, I stayed with my husband in his hiding place, high up in the attic of a barn full of hay. The first time I entered his humble home in the hay I saw a radio, which for the past several years we had been forbidden to possess. Every night we listened to the news from England and the parts of Holland that had already been freed by the Allies in September 1944 and were under Allied jurisdiction. When Ernst listened to the news from the radio station "Free Netherlands," he made notes and went out to tell other Jewish fugitives about it. The Queen of Holland would come on often to encourage the people in occupied Holland to be strong because the end of the war seemed to be in sight. This gave all those people who had been hiding, sometimes for three or even four years, hope for the future.

At the beginning of this terrible war, the Dutch royal family and their entourage fled to England. The Dutch population thought then that it was wrong for them to leave their people, but later it was clear that this was the wisest thing to do. Now the Queen could still be in contact with her government, which had also escaped to England. This made us feel safer than if she had stayed in her palace where she would have been forced by the Nazis to sign papers against her will. That is what happened to the King of Belgium who decided to stay home and live in his palace under the constant control of the German government. He had to sign humiliating laws protecting German war profits. After the war he was punished and had to cede the throne to his son. The populace never forgave him. They would rather have seen him in prison for resisting the Germans. We thought of him as having collaborated with the Germans by refusing to escape like our Queen.

Ernst was not of course supposed to have a radio; if the Nazis caught you with one, they picked you up and you were deported to a camp. But if we were caught as Jews in hiding, we would be deported anyway, so it didn't seem much of an added risk to own a radio. Even so, we were much less worried about deportation than we had been. The dangers were less intense than they had been before. The Nazis were still performing house searches to catch Jews and other fugitives, but less enthusiastically than in the beginning, knowing now that the war was lost. That is not to say they did not harm people, but if they did not receive specific orders to search for Jews or fugitives, they were not usually as inclined to do so on their own, as they had been earlier.

Nonetheless, there were still times when we could not sleep in our little place in the attic of the barn, especially when a really big *Aktion* was going on. At these times we would share a hiding place with some Jewish neighbours in a small shed way out in the fields. It was still on our host farmer's property, but nobody else around or in the village knew about this shed. There were a few bales of hay on the ground that we would move around the shed. Usually we took some blankets with us and stayed the night, sleeping until morning when the farmer gave us a sign that we could come out.

I remember one of these experiences of hiding in the shed as if it were yesterday. The phone message, in code of course, went around the neighbourhood and we immediately set out. We were soon joined by two more couples in this hiding place. It started to get dark, and after having worked all day, we were tired and made our bed ready. As usual we expected that nothing serious would happen to us. Nobody else knew about this place, did they? We rolled ourselves up in our blankets and tried to fall asleep. But, strangely enough, none of us could get warm and sleepy. The blankets were no help — the cold air penetrated right through them. We decided to walk around a little to warm our feet and hands, but nothing helped; we just grew colder and colder. This seemed so unnatural: it was autumn but the weather until now had been quite mild. We tried and tried to get warm, but to no avail. Finally we began asking one another whether we couldn't just go home to our different farms again. Surely the house searches would be over.

At this point, one of the men looked out the only little window in the shed. Suddenly he whispered that he saw a figure outside waving to us. We all jumped up to see and, yes, he was right. There in the dark was a vague figure waving to us, gesturing for us to come out. Of course we naturally assumed that it was one of the farmers telling us that we could come home again, and we went out. But we couldn't be sure who it was, for his face was hidden. Strangely, he did not lead us back to the farms but deeper into the fields. Then suddenly he stopped, pointed to a deep ditch newly lined with straw and gestured that we should go in. All at once we felt less cold for some reason. The figure stepped silently aside to let us pass, and we did what he wanted us to do. We jumped in, and turned around to thank him, naturally wanting to know who he was and why he wanted to help us. But when we turned around we were all astonished because there was nobody there. As far as we could see, there was nobody. How could he have disappeared so quickly?

This experience still puzzles me. Was it a man? A good friend? Or maybe an angel? I may never know the answer. I believe, though, that he was God-sent, because in less than an hour we heard Nazi voices screaming "*Raus, Raus,*" from the area we had just deserted. This miracle still gives me the trust that God will always protect us. We slept all through the night and awoke the next morning early, warm, and ready to return to our farms. The farm families were overcome with joy to see us again. Yes, the house searching had happened, and after finding no Jews in the farm houses, the Germans had gone straight to that little shed where we were hiding.

Another miracle occurred to some friends at the adjacent farm close by. These three people actually slept in the centre of what appeared to be a haystack, just for the night. It was a little wooden stall with one bed in it surrounded by bales of hay that had to be removed to allow entrance and exit. In fact, there were two haystacks, and they were hiding in one of them. Early in the morning we heard a bunch of trucks driving up to the farm and peeked out the window of the barn. Was it another house search? No, it appeared simply to be a group of soldiers and their leader on an exercise mission. Suddenly, they saw the two big haystacks next to each other — just what they wanted. Their job, it seemed, was to see how quickly they could take those apart and build them up again. Terrified, we watched them from our hiding place as their leader kept time on his watch as they dismantled the first haystack and then put it together again. When they were finished, the leader was satisfied, telling them that their time was excellent, and allowing the soldiers to smoke a cigarette.

But now, to our horror, he took out his watch and told the soldiers that it was time to take apart the other haystack, and to try to do this even quicker. Just when the soldiers got up and threw their cigarettes away, the well-known sound of the alarm system in the village went off — a shrill, piercing sound warning the citizens to get off the streets, because bomber airplanes were on their way to Germany and would fly over this village.

The soldiers went berserk. They knew that their trucks would give them away. So they all, including the commander, jumped into the ditches and behind bushes to get out of sight, hoping nothing would happen. The airplanes flew over and disappeared into the far distance. Then, a few minutes later, another alarm disturbed the silence telling them that they could come out now, that the danger was over. The soldiers came out of their hiding places and none of them, not even the commander, gave any more thought to tearing apart the remaining haystack, which of course would have revealed the family in hiding. They jumped in their trucks and hurried away.

Fifteen minutes later, the silence was broken again — this time by the sound of hay bales gently being pushed out of the other haystack where the people had been hiding. In a few seconds, out came a man and a woman and a child about ten years old.

White-faced and trembling, they made their path to the farm where the anxious and nervous family opened the door for them with all the love they had and all the thanks to God they could express. Was this episode a coincidence, as most people would say? Was it? We have to keep an open mind. We saw so many strange happenings and rescues for which there is no explanation.

As I have mentioned, when it became clear that Germany was losing the war, the Nazis virtually stopped looking for Jewish fugitives. What was the point in finding Jews now? What would they do with them besides send them to the already overcrowded concentrations camps? Besides, the soldiers by this time were so young, sometimes almost children, that we weren't particularly frightened of them. By the end of the war young boys of fourteen to sixteen years of age were called up to fight in Germany because there was so little manpower left — a pity to see such young people forced to fight. They too had mothers who did not like to see their boys taken from the house, knowing full well that they might never come home again.

Since it was now generally much safer in the neighbourhood than it had been, and because our host's farm was in an area of anti-Nazi farmers, I sometimes helped other families in the neighbourhood in addition to working for the Kelholts. I did sewing repairs and even made a few outfits. Because you could not buy any new clothes, you had to fix and mend the clothes you owned and darn the socks over and over. I made dresses out of material the farmer's wife received in return for traded food. At this time I could sew anything. Nothing was impossible for me to do as long as I was rewarded with food and a place to sleep. I would measure the women with a tape and then take a piece of newspaper and make a pattern, cut it out and away I went. Since I had little knowledge about how to construct a garment, the result was a dress that hung like a cloak, often longer in the back than in the front. But nobody ever complained; the farm people were not that fashionable and it was not a time to be picky.

In the severe winter of 1944–1945, the Germans already suspected that the war was lost, but fighting was still going on and the German army confiscated anything and everything that could be used to transport men and materials: bikes, wagons, wheelbarrows, cars. They also needed people. Especially in the towns and cities, the men were taken from their homes and set to work in factories in Germany while their poverty-stricken wives, mothers and children had to scavenge food for themselves.

In the cities that winter the food situation was chaotic and desperate. Food stamps were less and less useful. The stores could not get the food the city dwellers needed to survive, and very few people had enough money to purchase what these stores did stock. The town of Geesteren, near where we were hiding, was hit hard. The men who were forced to work in Germany did not receive wages, and the deserted wives' children often died from hunger. They were actually in much worse shape than we were. They tried to sell their belongings to the farmers in exchange for food, just to survive. Farmers were not usually in such dire straits. They had their own produce that they had grown, as well as milk, eggs, butter and a slaughtered pig or calf in a barrel or, if they could afford it, in an ice-box. Early in the morning, rain or shine, we saw people coming over the sandy roads, pushing baby carriages and wheelbarrows, simple self-constructed wooden carts heaped up with sheets, blankets, household articles and too many other things to recall. The smaller babies were pulled in makeshift wagons or were laid between the merchandise, while toddlers walked or helped by pushing or pulling. Their shoes were always worn through; some had no shoes at all. The mothers looked frail and white and could hardly walk for weakness. But they needed food for their children. Sometimes they walked for days from farm to farm, sleeping in barns at night, and then off again the next day to beg for a bit of food to sustain their children.

We lived in an area that was once a district of well-to-do farmers. Everybody we knew gave some food to these poor women and children. In the early morning Mrs. Kelholt took a piece of ham from the ceiling where it was hung to season and cut it into little blocks. A few eggs were added as well as a small piece of butter and a few potatoes or other produce. Finally about twenty little parcels were lying by the back door on the table to be handed out. Other farmers gave things such as bread, cheese and apples. Everybody gave something. The women would then travel from farm to farm collecting these little packages of food, and this way they had a better chance of surviving. The poor people would often offer blankets and other items in exchange, but the farmers didn't need them and would rarely take these things in exchange for the food they provided. The children needed their own bedding and clothes. The farmers simply could not take things from these poor people. After days of gathering supplies of food, these women had to go back to the city.

When these wives and children left the city, the Nazis did not try to stop them. In fact, they were often even friendly, bidding them a good trip. But it became difficult for the women to enter the city again, because the Nazis who watched the entrances into the cities were also very hungry. So, often, every little bit of food was taken away, and the poor people's trips were in vain. Therefore, to bring some food into the city, wives often hid the food in a ditch. Later, while one of the bigger children kept watch in the distance, the mother would return and tuck some of the hidden food under her clothes, keeping it against her bare body. Then she smuggled it to her home. Later, she would come back and do the same with more food. Sometime she would have to take a different road. They knew then that, along with the scarce food stamps, they could feed themselves again for a little while. After that food was gone, another trip would have to be made into the countryside.

And yet, this situation still did not signal the end of the war. Our clandestine radio connection made us aware that England and, in particular, London, was being hit with a great many missile attacks. A missile named V-2, an attack missile made under strict security, could be fired from northern Germany and could strike anywhere in England, causing great destruction. But based on the reports we heard from England, Prime Minister Churchill never gave up. He encouraged people by promising that Hitler would soon be defeated.

I should stress that I am no historian, but the way I recall it is that the final liberation of Holland occurred after the Canadian army cleared the Scheldt Estuary leading to Antwerp and the Allied army reinforced itself with more soldiers in the free south part of Holland in order to fight their way across the Rhine. After crossing the Rhine, the Canadian troops began entering Holland from the east.

Now events sped up. And it was not long before we saw the Canadian Allied soldiers marching through the highways and country roads, freeing everybody on their way. I can still see them coming through the main street of Geesteren, the closest town to where we were hiding. For the first time in two and a half years, I walked outside as Henriette Bollegraaf down the street in broad daylight into the town. The taste of freedom was indescribable; we had waited for it for so long.

Tall, handsome boys jumped off the vehicles, blowing us kisses and hugging the little babies in their mothers' arms. The soldiers handed out candy, cigarettes and so many other things, such as coffee, sugar and tea. We could not believe it. We were so excited because we hadn't seen these kinds of treats in ages. The farmers at that time had been making a kind of chicory coffee substitute. It was better than nothing but did not taste very good. I couldn't even remember the last time I had had a coffee. And thank God, the Canadians also had some medical supplies to give to the doctors and nurses.

CHAPTER 7

My Girls

How happy were we? It's difficult to put it down on paper. Elated. Is this the word? All words seem to fall short of the joy we felt in those first moments of freedom. All the Dutch citizens felt like one big family, and the many Jewish people who had not seen the sun or breathed the fresh air for years were completely speechless with joy. They were free; they could go to their homes again. Go to their families — whose whereabouts they did not yet know. They were all asking the same questions: where were their relatives and were they safe and healthy?

We could have gone home the same day if we wanted. We were free! But we remained at the farm until the end of June. The farmland had to be worked and my husband and I decided that — for all the help and support the Kelholt family had given us — we wanted to thank them by finishing the ploughing and seeding and other necessary seasonal chores. I still had to finish some sewing, which would take a few weeks. Our own future had to wait a while, and in fact we didn't have any plans for beginning our lives again. Nor did we know exactly how to resume our old lives from before the war. At the moment, we were in limbo.

As I think about it now, I realize that the first thought in my mind after learning of our freedom had nothing to do with sewing or extra work to thank the Kelholts. Rather, it was a burning desire to know where my baby girl Johanna was. It took about a week after our liberation to find out that she was living with a host family by the last name of Kingsma. Since the phones were connected again and no longer tapped, we could talk freely to her host family. In fact, she had been very close by, being looked after by a wealthy farming family. Of course we immediately prepared to go and see her. How was she? How big had she grown? Did she ever cry? Was she still blond? We climbed onto some borrowed bikes, feeling how wonderful it felt to ride over the highway without fear of arrest. In fact, it took me the longest time to get used to just walking or biking around. We had been hidden for so long. And there was no big yellow star hanging off our coats announcing that we were Jews. We were just normal people now. Free! With the summer sun warming our bodies and souls.

When we arrived at the farm, we were jubilant, yet shy too, about seeing Johanna after sixteen months. When the family greeted us at the door, I cried and kissed them and so did my husband. And when I looked over their shoulders into the hallway and living room, there was my baby, nearly a toddler, standing up and holding onto the seat of a chair and trying to shuffle to the next chair. She could not make it and fell on her little bum. But she got up right away without crying and tried again until she finally made it.

She had a lovely familiar face, my husband's features. They could not be missed. This little girl was surely ours; we did not need any tests to prove our parentage. My husband and I lifted her up and held her, but she didn't like it at all: strangers, people she did not know, kissing her. Her little lips trembled and now, for the first time, we heard her wail, certainly loud enough to wake people. We gave her over to the girl who had been taking care of her, and she immediately quieted down.

After our initial meeting, we all went down to the big kitchen. It had a very long table in the middle with at least fourteen to eighteen chairs ranged around it. We were invited to eat with the family. Seated already were two grown boys in work clothes, a teenage girl, and about nine children from twelve down to approximately three years of age. Our daughter, in the meantime, had been fed and put to bed for an afternoon nap. When everyone was seated, Mr. Kingsma came in, also in field clothes. He sat at the head of the table and gave the blessing before dinner, thanking the Lord for the abundance of food. Then serving dishes filled with vegetables, potatoes and meat were set in the middle in different places, so we could serve ourselves. We asked ourselves what was going on. Where was the mother of all those children? Once the conversation started we were soon able to tell the family about ourselves and which city we came from. We answered many more such questions, especially about being in hiding. At the end of the meal, the children disappeared to their rooms to do their homework or to play with the other kids in the surrounding farming neighbourhood. The grown-up boys returned again to the fields, leaving us behind in the kitchen with Mr. Kingsma. Finally, we could ask about the many children and the missing mother. He told us his story, about how he obtained our little girl, and why he, with all his own children, had taken her in.

He had married his first wife when he was a young man. They were happy together and she gave birth to two healthy boys. But when after several years his wife died of cancer, he became depressed and could not look after the boys, who were still children. They needed a mother. Luckily, he soon found another woman he could love. Not long after, however, sickness also entered this relationship, and, worse, something went wrong with the birth of their daughter. The baby was healthy, but the mother, as often happened before antibiotics were discovered, died of an infection a few days after giving birth.

Now he had three children who needed a mother. He became desperate: how could he look after those young children when he had to make a living working all day in the fields? After trying out various housekeepers without much success, he found himself a third mate. This lady was young and healthy and she soon became a devoted mother. And, being Catholic, she also wanted children of her own. So, about every twelve to fourteen months his wife became pregnant. She was a sturdy woman with powerful hands. She sewed and cooked and was in every way a devoted mother. Each successive year brought healthy boys and girls until about nine or ten were born. The father did not mind since he was wealthy with a large amount of livestock and fertile fields, which produced good crops of wheat and vegetables. And there was always room for more hands to work on the farm.

But calamity struck the Kingsma family yet again. After giving birth to her last child, his wife began to feel ill. When she went to the doctor she was diagnosed with tuberculosis. It was not too serious yet, but the doctor told her that she must rest, that she must stay away from other people, and that she should definitely not have another child right away. With proper care and enough fresh air, she would get better. So there she was, outside all day long trying to get better in a sort of wooden tent that could be turned, because the sun was not allowed to shine on her. When the sun went on its way through the sky, the tent, along with her bed, was wheeled around by a member of their family, keeping her out of direct sunshine as the doctor had ordered. At night, she slept in the house. Because she had been prohibited from having another child, she and her husband decided to take in a Jewish baby. Being religious people, they felt it was an honour to God to do so. We were very moved by this story. This man had suffered so much in losing two wives, and now his third wife was lying outside alone with T.B., and yet he was so kind to us.

My baby was blond and fair-skinned and could really have been one of the Kingsmas' own children. The resemblance was so close that they both had decided to make the birth official by registering her under their family name in their municipality. Also, when the neighbours received the invitation to see the new family member and brought gifts to congratulate the couple, they were all astonished at how much this child resembled the farmer or one of the other members of his family. If we had not come back they would have raised and loved this baby as their own, and nobody would ever have known the truth. How strange that of all the children I would have, Johanna was the only blond one. By birth, the other seven had dark hair and brown eyes. Even now, I am convinced that a miraculous force saved her life and ours.

After Mr. Kingsma's explanation, we went outside to the back yard and met the mother. We thanked her very much. We could not come too close to her, for fear of catching T.B., but we were sitting close enough that we could talk to each other. She told us more about the baby, how smart she was already, what foods she liked, her habits of sleeping and all those things we did not know much about. While we stayed at the Kelholts we often went to see Johanna, since the Kingsma family lived a mere bike ride away. She quickly got used to us and soon we could hold her and play with her, without her being upset and crying. Despite her growing accustomed to us, we resolved not to take her away from the family right away, realizing how upsetting such a move could be for her. Besides, it would be difficult to look after her while we were still working at the Kelholt's farm. The Kingsmas were happy to keep her as long as possible.

At the end of June 1945, Ernst and I decided to move back to Amersfoort. We knew we had to settle ourselves before we could have Johanna with us. We also wanted to begin looking for my other daughter, Elly. It felt so strange to go back. We were returning to our hometown, but we were starting over as if it were a brand new place. Initially we did not have a place to live in Amersfoort. We could not move back to my sister Henny's house, nor to the house owned by Ernst's family. Other people were already living there. Instead, we moved in with a couple of older ladies who had never married, the two Miss Van Beek sisters. They kindly opened their home to us and we stayed for about a month. Since

Ernst's family warehouse had been around the corner from where they lived, he had been acquainted with them before the war. Their father had a business in making chairs and knew Ernst's father quite well. This craftsman had since passed away, but the two ladies remained in the house.

In August we went to a bureau and, with the help of the Underground, were set up with a very small house to rent. It was a row house, smaller than small and barely furnished. But it was enough. What with the ongoing help of the Resistance organizations and the municipalities, many people found new housing after the war. It certainly helped that there was not a huge demand for housing; there were simply not that many immigrants coming into Holland. And there were always little cubbyholes that were available for rent here and there. We rented our tiny home for what amounted to six dollars a week. Every Monday morning the bell would ring: six dollars, please. When we were finally settled in our little house, it was time to sever the bonds between Johanna and her host family. It was difficult to take Johanna away from the loving Kingsma family, but she belonged with us. The farewell was heart-wrenching. They really had raised her from a baby of two months to a toddler of sixteen months. When we finally waved good-bye, everyone in the family was crying, and so were we. We continued to visit them occasionally and learned that Mrs. Kingsma eventually became well again.

In the meantime, my two sisters and their families returned from their places of hiding. The Underground also arranged rental housing for them, but the two families now lived in separate row houses, not together as they had before the war and for part of their time in hiding. Their experiences during the war had been even more hazardous than ours, especially because, as I mentioned earlier, my brother-in-law Bram suffered greatly in the war, having had one of his legs amputated. Because he removed his prosthesis in bed at night, he could not always be so quick in escaping to their hiding places. When the warning came, he had trouble disappearing in time. Henny also related some nerve-racking experiences about hiding in corn fields with Arnold and the children while the Nazis were searching the farm where they were staying. But at least they were both able to keep their families together in hiding and appeared to have had kind and generous host families. Even now Jo receives visitors from the family that they stayed with in hiding, although these days it's their children and grandchildren who visit.

We were overjoyed to have my sisters back. Their return also meant that my oldest daughter, Elly, might have survived. I can never be thankful enough to Jo and Bram who helped me so much with her. They were thrilled to see us too, and they had news of Elly. They explained that during the last two years, things had become so dangerous that they had been forced to give Elly up to another family while they were in hiding. It must have hurt them to do so because they had come to love her so much, having raised her from a baby until that point. Elly's host family lived in the outskirts of Mechelen, a mining town about forty miles west of Maastricht. I was eager to travel there with my husband to see Elly again and bring her home with us.

Somehow I don't remember the husband of Elly's host family, but the wife seemed to be a friendly lady and welcomed us. They had seven boys and two girls. All of these nine children were considerably older than Elly. Some of them were already working. One of the younger sons, Johan, who had a particularly friendly attitude with the young children, would sometimes tow Elly in a wagon when he was not in school. Most of the children in this family had straight light-brown hair, whereas Elly's hair was dark brown and very curly. In no way did she resemble any of the other children, or the parents. Since hiding Elly inside the house was impossible — she was too young to accept confinement — she lived in the open as if she were part of the family, even though it was quite noticeable that she did not look the part. The family must have experienced many anxious moments wondering what would happen to them if they were discovered "hiding" a Jewish child. However, in the little mining town of Mechelen, part of free

Holland after September 1944, none of the townspeople said a word.

Despite the relative safety of her situation with the family, it became clear to us when we saw Elly that she had suffered quite a bit. Her feet, I noticed, were abnormally small, which I later found out was due to that fact that her host family had never bought her new shoes. Her baby shoes caused her feet to cramp up. She also had chronic bronchitis from living in a cold environment.

I don't think Elly's host family had meant to be negligent about her health. During the war they had themselves suffered extreme financial hardships and must have done the best they could under the harsh circumstances. They owned a little inn along the main road, which allowed them to serve beer and put up guests. But the Germans made all kinds of rules, and these rules made it very difficult for them to earn a living. For example, there was the law that after eight o'clock at night nobody could be out on the streets. Initially, these street bans were for Jewish people. But later, during the bombing raids, the Dutch had to adhere to the curfews as well. When nightfall came, the Dutch were also supposed to be inside with no lights showing. For an inn that depended on late-night customers, these laws were disastrous.

But I have to say that there were also other problems with Elly's host family. The mother seemed pleasant enough, but the relationship between her and her husband appeared troubled and turbulent. Elly remembers a time when the man chased his wife with a knife. While he probably wouldn't really have done anything to his wife or the children, such behaviour frightened and upset Elly.

Even with all these difficulties with the host family, I have to say that when we came to get Elly, she did not want to leave. She may not have been in the best of situations, but she was familiar with it. She knew about me, but she didn't remember me and did not know Ernst at all. To her, we were strangers. She had received the rag doll that I had sent her and loved playing with it; she knew that it was from me, but she hadn't seen me since she was three. And even before that, my sister Jo was more of a mother to her than I was. She had grown up with Jo, and even now sees Jo as her second mother. She was suspicious and wary of us. "I'm not going with you," she informed me. "Why not?" I asked. "Because you won't bring me back," she responded. Initially she was determined to stay with what she knew, even if it was not the most positive or nurturing environment, rather than venture into what she did not know — living with us.

Surprisingly, I wasn't terribly upset or heartbroken that Elly didn't remember me or want to come with us when we came to visit her. To be honest, she was so grown up at five I could hardly remember her anymore either. At the time we were reconciled to her, she was nearly old enough to go to public school. So much had happened. As with my daughter Johanna, we decided not to take her with us right away, but to visit her a few times first. The host family was kind, despite their shortcomings, and were content to keep Elly with them for this transitional time. They were attached to her too. And it needs to be said that this family risked their lives for Elly. We have never forgotten them. Neither should the other families who hid Jews and other fugitives during the war be forgotten. They put their own lives in danger to save ours. When Elly finally came back to us after the war, the first thing I did was make her some new clothes and buy some shoes that fit her. I continued to do a lot of sewing. In Amersfoort there was an excellent yard goods shop called Beretz and Lange. They gave us many sample materials and leftover pieces, as well as sewing and knitting needles, and yarn. For small children you could do a lot with these leftovers.

After we settled into our home, we had our religious Jewish wedding ceremony. Like our other wedding ceremony, it was small. Just a few friends and the rabbi. We had the Jewish prayers. As part of the ceremony we would each drink some wine out of the same wine glass and, when the ceremony ended, it was part of the ritual to put the glass on the floor and for the husband to stomp on it. The shattering of the glass meant that no one could put it back together again — symbolizing that the marriage needed to remain intact and whole. I must say that this ceremony wasn't particularly meaningful to me. We had already been officially married for three years and we had a family. But we were Jewish. We felt it had to be done, that it was expected of us. So we did it for the sake of tradition.

After the religious marriage, we tried hard to settle permanently into our new existence in our old hometown of Amersfoort. It should have been a life of freedom with no fear of being arrested or sent to a concentration camp. And yet we felt lost. Where were our parents, my husband's sister, her husband and children, my brother and his wife, and their twins? Three months had elapsed since the end of the war. They should have been back in the city. Right after the war, when the concentration camps were liberated, the prisoners in the camps were often transported to hospitals or holding camps. Only very occasionally were they brought home right away, and this only if they were strong enough. So we didn't expect our families back immediately. We knew that it might take a few months for them to come home. Everybody hoped for the best, but the more we hoped and speculated, the harder the truth was when it came.

As weeks passed, our expectations of seeing our family alive changed to worry and distress. It was taking them far too long to come home; the concentration camps were empty and they were not on any of the hospital, holding camp, or refugee camp lists. The Underground kept checking for us. Eventually there were only a few names trickling in. And those names were not members of our family. We began to realize the worst. Finally nobody was left. They were not coming back. The happy family reunion we had anticipated — that had helped us through our toughest times in hiding — was nothing more than our own imaginings and hopes. Everyone who had been freed when the Allied forces liberated the camps was now home or in a hospital to recover. During the war we were not sure what life for the prisoners in the concentration camps had been like — whether they worked in factories or in the fields. We had heard some whispers of their being killed and burned to ashes, but we always thought that this could not be true. Even Nazis could not kill and burn so many prisoners. We knew that they could be cruel, but this? No, we could not believe it.

The news about the concentration camps slowly filtered through to us in Holland. There were no big headlines about the camp atrocities in Poland and elsewhere. It tended to be more word of mouth. We were completely shocked when we began to hear the stories; we had no idea of the extent to which the Nazis had gone in terminating millions of lives. We knew there were transports to concentration camps. But it was couched in positive terminology, mostly in terms of there being work in the camps for the people. We had no idea that the kind of work that they had to do — that is, if they weren't gassed right away — would slowly kill the workers. We assumed the conditions were tolerable, that people were often employed in their area of expertise, and that they might even be getting some money for their labour.

I think a lot of people in Holland just didn't know. Or maybe they did . . . ? No, I don't really believe the average person knew much at all. Those of us who had been in hiding for the last two and a half years of the war had no clue. The Jewish Council must have known about it, and certainly the political parties in Holland, perhaps even some of the city dwellers, but for us in hiding, we knew nothing of the mass extermination during the war. Nor did the Dutch make a big deal of the death camps in Poland after the war. The war had damaged so much of the population — soldiers who had died, women and children who had starved — that most people were trying to get over their own grief and didn't have room for more. What was a handful of Jews among the entire population? The horrors in the concentration camps were linked directly to the horrors of war that hit almost every family in the country, not as a unique, predominately Jewish massacre. In Holland, we didn't hear anything about "remembering" those who perished in the Holocaust. There were no memorials. It was only later that these forms of mourning began. What we felt or experienced wasn't labelled anything; we hadn't heard of the term "trauma."

Once it began to sink in what had happened, we talked about the deportation a lot, and cried for the losses in our family. I think of the three of us, my sister Jo had the most difficulty dealing with the loss of our parents. She and my father were very close; they were like two peas in a pod. They had often talked together and really seemed to understand each other. By the time I was born, my parents were already much older, so I don't think I got to know them in quite the same way.

Working through a difficult situation takes time. It doesn't happen right away, even after talking about it together. Time has helped to heal these losses, but the scars and the longings never disappear. Even now I have times when I want nothing more than to go home to my parents' house and say, "Hi Mom! Hi Dad!" And sit together, feeling safe and loved in their care. That desire has never gone away. We often looked at the photographs of my parents and of my brother, Simon, his wife and their lovely twins, who were about eleven years old when I saw them last. As I think I mentioned earlier, a deported Jew who returned from Auschwitz told us that he had known my brother, but not his wife or children. Simon had been allowed to work, until he died of starvation, over-exhaustion and typhus. We never found out if he had played his violin when the poor people had been led to the gas chambers. We had heard that an orchestra often played to show the newcomers on their arrival that nothing was wrong, that they were on their way to a building to have a shower and receive fresh clothing. Yet as I think about the story now, I wonder how they could have believed in a rosy future when the heavy smoke that was coming out of the crematorium took their breath away. What horrifying cruelty. I cannot fathom it.

It was terrible when I realized that my family wasn't coming back. At the same time, I wouldn't let myself fall into a depression. I had a life to create for myself, my husband and my children. I didn't want to become lost in the past and the pain. We had all lost people. My pain could not be worse than theirs. We lost our parents and my brother, but my Uncle Jan lost his children. That was much worse. To lose a parent, even in a horrible and untimely way, is more in the natural order of things than to lose a child. Uncle Jan suffered intensely from the emotional pain of the loss of his sons. Can you die from heartache? It would seem so.

Even though I tried to bury the pain, I recognize that this sadness has been with us our entire lives. On every happy occasion, as when one of our children graduated from school or university, or was married, even when my husband and I needed some advice, we have missed our parents' presence. Our lives will never be complete. A great gap remains. My children never knew their grandparents; my husband and I became orphans when we were in our mid-twenties. Over the years I have experienced many bouts of depression and have had a hard time getting over them. Even the knowledge that most of the Dutch people who assisted the Nazis in gathering and transporting the Jews were imprisoned for being collaborators cannot bring our family back again. They were reduced to ashes and billowing smoke clouds, or thrown into mass graves. But now, having an extended family — children, grandchildren, and even great grandchildren — has helped me to regain some of my joy.

. We sisters became closer after the war was over. We had to because there was basically no one left from the rest of our family. We met together once or twice weekly to drink coffee, play cards and just talk. As there were very few Jewish people in Amersfoort after the war, we felt quite isolated. Of the 820 Jews that had lived there in 1941, very few returned after the war. Actually, there weren't many Jewish people left in Holland, period. I learned that of the 140,000 Dutch Jews who had been living in Holland before the war, roughly 107,000 were deported and an estimated 5,200 survived the Holocaust. In 1946, only 30,000 Jews lived in Holland, and many of them decided to emigrate to North America or Palestine. There was still a synagogue in Amersfoort but there were not many attendees; there was only a very small Jewish community that met together. All my Jewish friends from childhood and my working life were gone. I had had Dutch friends in public school, but I was never close enough to them to renew our friendship after the war. Jo had one good friend whom she met again after the war. In fact, she remained friends with her for many years until the woman passed away. But I desperately missed having a community of people so that we could meet together and social-ize, so that we could enjoy each other's company and throw our-selves into intense discussions. We were home again in Amersfoort, but it was never really home for us. There was so little left to make it home.

The Dutch government tried to compensate us for our losses. A number of the leading Dutch Nazi perpetrators were prosecuted, and some, like Dr. Arthur Seyss-Inquart, the Reich Commissioner in Holland, were tried and hanged for their crimes, while others were sentenced to life imprisonment. Also, in August 1945, a spe-cial organization called the Council for the Restitution of Legal Rights was created. Its goal was to restore the legal rights of the dispossessed and also to return to them or their heirs the property, real estate, art objects, etc., that had been taken from them. But most of us received minimal compensation. Although our legal rights were restored and anti-Semitism was no longer blatant, we lost virtually everything of monetary value in the war: heirlooms, money, family treasures. Much more devastating to us was the loss of our families, our friends, our community, and part of our own lives. How could we possibly be compensated?

The war and the Holocaust turned our lives totally upside down. My nursing career was permanently on hold, and after having given birth to more children after the war I could not expect to get my diploma. Initially, when we moved back, Ernst tried to reopen the recycling business that he and his father owned before the war, but it was impossible. The company had been taken over by Nazi collaborators during our absence and was now bankrupt. The gov-ernment was not much help. To start a business you needed money and we didn't have any. We were told, however, that we could have the old building back to start again. When we went to the taxation office and asked for information about the income of my in-laws, to our surprise, it seemed that my father-in-law had not been a completely honest bookkeeper. Ernst and I had been led to believe that the business was prosperous. But the books showed otherwise. In fact, it appeared that the business had a deficit rather than a surplus of funds. When we went to the tax office to find financial statements so we could obtain a bank loan to set up the business again, they nearly threw my husband in jail because he had been a partner with his father. He tried to explain that it was his father who had looked after the books and that, as his son, he received only a salary. At the time he was only in his early twenties and knew nothing about the financial transactions. They let him off the hook, but the result was that the government would not help us regain the old business. And without any money, we could not start again alone. We had come back to Amersfoort with no money at all.

One of the first things we did when we returned was go to the neighbouring families who had agreed to store our furniture and money until we returned. Some of them did return our things. We were able to retrieve our old grandfather clock and our desk from the Boers, and a few other things that we left with some other families. Many people and acquaintances, however, had been changed by the war. We saw that often they had become dishonest and cheated each other. Could we blame them for this? They all had their own families to raise, and how could you do this during the war if you did not fight for it? Mrs. Boer, for instance, returned our furniture, but when we wanted our family linens and blankets back, she told us that she had been forced to sell them in order to survive the war. Things had been so bad in Holland that many people sold their items in the streets in order to have enough money to buy some food. We had seen this desperate poverty in Geesteren. So I thought, "Okay, if you had to sell them to survive, that's fine. I would have wanted you to do that." A few weeks later we made a visit to this same family. Mrs. Boer was sick and we visited her in the bedroom. There she was, lying between my mother-in-law's sheets, with our family blankets on top of her. It was obvious because my mother-in-law's initials were sewn right on them.

Another family had been storing some household items, valuables, money and jewellery that Ernst's parents left with them before they were deported. Since the Bollegraafs were well known in the neighbourhood, these neighbours had been willing to hide their valuables in their houses so that they would be there when the Bollegraafs returned. Ernst's parents thought this was a generous offer and took them up on it, happily and thankfully. When we realized that we needed some of the items in order to set up housekeeping, and we knew for sure that our parents were not coming back to us, we asked for them back. They refused, saying that it was too bad that Ernst's parents had not returned, but that the goods belonged to my in-laws and we had no right to use them. "No," they said stubbornly, "we'll wait for your parents." Which did not make much sense since they also indicated that the money and other items they had kept for Ernst's parents were virtually gone. They had used them to buy food to survive. We got nothing back from them.

Thankfully we still had the business money and some jewellery hidden in the home of the grocer, behind a tile in their kitchen. Or so we thought. We hurried over to their home. But when we arrived, they told us, "Oh, you already sent somebody to pick it up! We don't have it." But we never did. They swore high and low that we had sent someone already. How could this be? We were the only ones who knew the money was there. And be reasonable, what were we to do with jewels and gold if we could not even show ourselves on the street? We didn't need much, just a little furniture and money. But we did not make a court case out of it. What was there for proof? Their word against ours. And how could we pay the court if we did not have any money to pay for a lawyer? Despite these losses, we were still optimistic — we had each other and we were young. In the end, we collected some old furniture from various crisis centers. But it did hurt that people could change character so much in a few years.

Jo and Henny and their families went through the same agony. Jo had left some curtains and drapes with friends, and when she went over to retrieve them, the curtains were openly hanging in their windows. "Yes," they said, "you can have them back if you have some other ones for us." It was all so ridiculous. Finally we gave up and made do with what we owned ourselves. A very meagre start, but I tried to be positive. The years after the war were incredibly difficult. The war itself was five years, but for us, and we were not the only Jews who were cheated this way, the war years plus the after-effects totalled more than ten years.

We weren't the only ones in the poor house. The Dutch government, which was in exile during the war, could do almost nothing to ease the financial burdens that the German occupation caused. Dutch produce had been shipped to Germany and all Dutch industry had been geared towards the war effort. Consequently, after the war almost everybody was poor. On top of this there was high inflation in Holland, so money had little value. Too much had been printed. Even the wartime black market dealers lost out, since all their stacked-away money was now just coloured paper. Things became so bad after the war that Holland finally introduced a new currency. We each received ten guilders from the government. It does not seem much now, but those ten guilders were most welcome. If I was careful, we could live on ten guilders for almost two weeks.

Much help came from surrounding countries like Sweden and Switzerland, the countries whose economy had not been completely turned upside down during and after the war. In addition, between 1948 and 1954, Holland received over one billion American dollars as part of the U.S. Marshall Plan. By the mid-1950s things were virtually stable again. But I recall vividly the period of shortages after the war when we first began to receive white flour, powdered eggs, canned meats, butter, powdered milk and many more things that most people had not seen in more than three or four years. It was a sign of hope when the butcher shops opened again, although there was only a small supply of meat. Since the stores were not fully stocked right away, the meat was rationed. Livestock had disappeared and so, alarmingly, had dogs and cats. We could not imagine what had happened to them. When I went to do our shopping, the butcher shops and the bake shops were regularly sold out. So, often, I went to the slaughterhouse where they sold beef and pork over the counter, meat from animals which had not passed the grade to be sold in the stores.

It is interesting to remember how this was done. The animal was first cut in square blocks and each block was put into a bag. You never knew what you would receive. Sometimes, if you were lucky, it was a sirloin steak, but more often we ended up with meat that was so tough it was good only for soup or for slicing up thin enough to make sandwiches. Often there were more bones than meat. I was always thankful for what I received, but in order to return home with one of these bags of treasure, I had to wait several hours in line while Johanna was alone at home. I often had to leave my baby in her crib napping and, while standing in line, I was usually torn between waiting for my turn and running home to see what she was doing. Like many other mothers in the same position, we were nervous about our babies being alone at home. Fortunately, everything was usually fine, and I could breathe again when I returned home.

Ernst could not take any time off work to help watch the children. Being unable to rebuild his old business, he started working for another recycling company in Hilversum. This company wanted Ernst to work for them because he was so knowledgeable in the trade, but he had to travel back and forth to the workplace, an hour each way. He had to get up very early in the morning and he arrived home late at night. He earned a salary there of perhaps ninety guilders a month. It was enough to survive, but we lived mostly hand to mouth. He worked there for over a year while we tried to get our feet back on the ground.

Finally in early 1947 Ernst managed to start up his own business again. We began by renting our old warehouse. There were certain restrictions for people wanting to go into business that we had to overcome. You had to prove that you were an expert in the field and convince the bank that you had enough money to cover your expenses for two years, in case things went belly up. But at that time, these restrictions were not heavily imposed; there was room to manoeuvre because of the general economic hardships through-out the country. Because of these relaxed restrictions, we were able to open the business without having to go through the whole financial rigmarole that was normally necessary.

Still, to run a successful recycling business, we needed to have money up front. People would come with a cart full of scrap metal, and we would have to pay them on the spot. In the beginning we received some help from a Jewish man who was also in the scrap business. He was wealthy and willing to lend us money when we needed it. He had also gone into hiding but had been able to regain some of his wealth after the war. He liked my husband quite a bit, and I guess he felt sorry for us. Perhaps he also wanted to help out his fellow Jews after all the hardships our people had experienced. Whatever the reason, he always gave us assistance when we needed it. We also had a young apprentice helping Ernst. A Jewish woman had come to our house and told us she had a nephew who had survived the concentration camps and was now interested in learning the recycling business. She asked if we would be willing to take him on as an apprentice in our business. He would work for us and we would look after him and allow him to live with us. We agreed.

Slowly Ernst began building up his clientele. But it was no easy task. It had been almost five years since he had been in the business, and things never did take off after the war as they had before. Other recycling and scrap businesses had developed while we were in hiding, and those customers who had been ours previously were going to the new places when Ernst came back on the scene.

Around that time, maybe late 1947, we thought about going to Germany, where the Bollegraaf recycling business had started. As

I mentioned earlier, Ernst's father and mother had made their start in the German town of Bunde by shipping recycling materials to different factories in both Germany and Holland. Eventually they had expanded their business to include the warehouse in Amersfoort. Ernst had grown up in Bunde and was familiar with the town and the surrounding area. And more importantly, he still had the family house and warehouse there. And so it was that we made a trip to Germany to see how things were, how the économy was, and if we could get our house and warehouse back. When we arrived in Bunde, the Germans treated us amazingly well. They remembered Ernst from before the war and of course they remembered the Bollegraaf family. "Come in, come in. I'm so glad you're back," was the common welcome around town. Everyone was inviting us over for coffee. They were happier to see us than the people in Amersfoort were when we came back after our two and a half years of hiding.

Other people now lived in the house, of course, and they used the warehouse for a different business. Because we legally owned the property, we could have demanded that they leave, but when we saw their faces nearly begging us to let them stay, we could not do that. Besides, when we looked at the situation in Germany, we were not sure it would be wise to stay. True, in time we would have received some *Wiedergutmachen* (money from the government), but we saw that things were not normal in Germany yet. People had suffered incredible losses. There were many sad situations in which families had been torn apart. So many young people had been forced to serve in the army, with countless numbers having been killed for doing their duty. Numerous people invited us to come into their homes and meet what was left of their family. We visited one elderly lady whose three sons, who were childhood friends of Ernst's, had not returned after the war. She still hoped that one or more would return because the only message that she had received was that they were "lost in action." She longed for a reunion and every day baked cookies and strudel, food that her boys loved. But not one returned home. When we saw her it was almost three years after the war and she was still baking, waiting and waiting.

It is my belief that we have to feel pity for these mothers too. After all, they did not want the war. They loved their children just as much as we did. They could not have known that the Nazi regime would be so dangerous, and that the war would have such devastating results. In fact, not many of Ernst's school friends were alive any more. We heard so many distressing stories that we decided not to go back to Bunde to live. We could not handle more sadness. Later on, we decided to sell the house and the warehouse. We arranged with the people living in it that they could buy both the house and the warehouse for a lump sum. They agreed and were pleased not to have to leave.

In the meantime our little family was growing bigger and bigger. By 1949 we had three more girls: Betty was born in 1946, Tikki in 1947, and Carla in 1949. Betty and Tikky were both born in the hospital. It was becoming much more common for women to have children in the hospital at that time. There was less risk than with a home-birth because the medical staff could catch problems and infections much more easily and quickly than a midwife could. When Tikky was born, I didn't want to name her. I was upset that I had four girls. I had wanted a boy. But Ernst had to go to the town hall to register her within forty-eight hours after she was born. And to register her, she needed a name. So Ernst decided to name her after us: Henriette Ernestine. Betty was just over one year old at the time and adored her baby sister. But unable to say her name, she called her "Tikky." The name stuck.

Carla was named after my mother, Kaatje. Since Kaatje was a rather old-fashioned name, we modernized it a bit. I gave birth to Carla at home with a midwife and ended up with an infection after her birth because the midwife was not conscientious about sanitation. Soon after the birth I came down with a fever that lasted for at least a week. I had wanted to have Carla in the hospital, too, but Ernst couldn't take me because when I went into labour he was in bed with a concussion from a motorcycle accident. He had

gone to Germany to see some friends and on the way home the
bike skidded on a wet street. How he got home, I'll never know.
All I know is that he was blue when he stumbled in the door. I was
just thankful that he was alive. After his concussion, Ernst had the
bike fixed and decided to sell it. But before he put it up for sale
he wanted to take it for a spin around the neighbourhood to
make sure it was okay. He came to an intersection and had a col-
lision. Now he was in bed with a broken leg. Between looking
after four girls and a newborn and Ernst in and out of bed, it was
an eventful time to say the least.

Ernst was always a supportive husband and father, but he didn't
really have a strong fatherly feeling and loved to go out and have
a good time. For fun we would go out dancing. We were still
young, in our late twenties. My husband was a great dancer, especially at the tango. Could we ever move. There wasn't really such
a thing as baby sitters at that time, so Elly would be in charge. But
since she was only eight or nine, we would ask the lady next door
to pop in from time to time to check on the girls and make sure
they were all right. Neighbours were always quick to help each
other.

Ernst tended to be much more social than I was. When we
moved back to Amersfoort, Ernst seemed to pick up his social life
right where he left off and appeared to adjust much more easily
to our circumstances after the war than I did. He was a good tennis player — he was left- and right-handed so he could do anything with a tennis racket — and joined the tennis club again. He
promptly became acquainted with all the girls at the tennis club,
while I was sitting at home with two, later three, and then four
kids. One Sunday my sister Jo came over and asked, "Where's
Ernst?" "Oh, he's off playing tennis," I answered. She replied,
"You're crazy! Put your coat on; we'll take the kids with us. We're
going to see what he's up to." So we bundled up the girls in the
wagon and one in the carriage and went off to the tennis courts,
which were not very far away. When we neared the courts we
could hear lots of gabbing and giggling. Ernst was playing tennis

with a load of girls. We stood along the side of the courts waving and shouting, "Hi! Hello!" Then one of the girls asked Ernst, "Who is that?" "Oh," he replied casually, "that's my wife and children." They had no idea he was married. I didn't get jealous easily and thought it was quite funny; I don't think Jo found it nearly as humorous.

For six years we stayed in our smaller-than-small rented home. It was on a quiet street on the outskirts of Amersfoort where the children could play on the sidewalk. When I think about the spacious apartment that I live in today, I have no idea how we squeezed so many people into that little place. We had five girls in a two-bedroom home. My husband and I slept in one room, four of the girls slept in the other room, and Elly had her own tiny room that was really more like a closet off our bedroom, just big enough for a bed. It was a tall, two-storey house with an attic as well, but had no width and was not at all roomy.

As I remember the house now, everything seems rather old-fashioned compared to what we have today. We had a gas oven but no fridge. We didn't even have an icebox, so there was no cold storage for eggs, meats, and cheeses. I tended to buy the food we needed for the day. Of course some vegetables, like potatoes and onions didn't have to be refrigerated. We could keep them for weeks. We also didn't have a modern bathroom with a bathtub and sink in it. Just a small room with a toilet. By this time of course the more modern apartments were equipped with flush toilets with a pull chain. Once a week on bath day I would have all the girls sit on the kitchen counter while I'd fill the sink full of hot water and put some soap on the side. Then each girl would take a bath. My husband would take a shower with a pail of warm water outside the warehouse after he did his work in the scrap yard. But we still ended up with a lot of fleas in the house from his dirty clothes. Since we did not know the latest technology we didn't feel as though we were missing out on anything. Who could imagine how much things would change?

The Ankersmit Family who first hid Rhodea and her husband on their farm in 1943. It was here that Rhodea's daughter Johanna was born. LEFT TO RIGHT: Mr. Ankersmit, Heintje, Rÿn, Mrs. Ankersmit.

The Kelholt family, who hid Rhodea and her husband until the end of the war. Rhodea, Mina, Gerrit, Reintje, Jan, Rhodea's husband Ernst.

Members of the Dutch resistance guard fellow countrymen accused
of collaborating with the Germans during the occupation,
Nijmegen, Sept. 20, 1944. Courtesy of the United States
Holocaust Memorial Museum.

The population of Amsterdam cheers as the first elements
of the Canadian Army enter the Dutch capital on
VE Day, May 8, 1945.

Rhodea's two daughters, Johanna (l.) and Elly (r.), who were
born during the war (1945).

The Bollegraaf family arrived in Canada from Holland
aboard the *Volendam*, October 1951.

CHAPTER 8

Bon Voyage

During the late 1940s and early '50s, we kept hoping that we would be able to create stability for ourselves and our family, but we could not find a way to achieve this. Ernst's recycling business wasn't operating well enough for us to see a future in it. Even the huge industrial expansion in Holland after the war, including the manufacture of steel, transportation equipment and large machinery, did not make much of a difference to our small business. While the business was relatively stable, it was too small and did not offer much financial security. Jo and Bram seemed to be managing reasonably well. Although Bram was an invalid and had been unable to find a job immediately after the war, the newly installed Dutch government helped him and rewarded his efforts in the army with an allowance and an office position in a kind of national lottery. This job paid well, was not too difficult, and allowed him to work sitting. When Bram and Jo had saved enough money, they bought a home downtown with a front room that opened onto the street. This room became an office where people could come and buy their lottery tickets. That way he didn't have to travel to work. Jo had two more children after the war, a girl and a boy. She had her boy right at the time when I had one of my girls, and Ernst joked that we should trade because we already had two girls and were long overdue for a boy. Arnold and Henny also seemed to have pulled their lives together. Arnold was able to get back into his business as an entrepreneur and they also had a son after the war. Ernst must have been feeling jealous by this time.

During our time in Holland before the German invasion, we had enjoyed relatively good living conditions and had believed we could raise our children in a comfortable fashion. The war and the horrors experienced by our family, friends and the Jewish community had collapsed our sense of security and community. We now felt that to put the past behind us and to make a future for ourselves in Holland would be an overwhelming task mentally and emotionally. I even felt negative feelings emanating from some people, which gave me the impression that they wished we had stayed away after the war. Whether these were their actual sentiments or not, I don't know. All I knew is that I wanted to start afresh, somewhere far away from our pain and our memories — somewhere completely new, in a land of opportunity where there would be no threat of dictatorship.

In the early 1950s the newspapers and radio announced repeatedly that Canada needed people. It was a vast and empty country, they said, with no more than fourteen million people. We learned that the Canadian government had made a contract with Holland to allow Dutch families to immigrate to their immense country. Was this not a terrific possibility? Holland had little room for opportunity and, since most of our family and friends were gone, we had little keeping us. The more we thought about it, the more we remembered the friendly faces and the generosity of the Allied forces, in particular the Canadian soldiers who had liberated parts of Holland and had ridden through the streets of Geesteren. Besides the Nazis, these were the only soldiers that we had met personally. Even before knowing very much about Canada, our hearts began to yearn for this country which seemed to offer a chance to better ourselves through hard work and new relationships, a chance for our children to grow up away from our tortured memories. Gradually the picture of Canada became clearer and clearer in our minds. It would have wide open fields, a nice home or a farm with a vegetable garden, children fetching eggs every morning and the entire family eating them with our breakfast. I envisioned Canada as a Garden of Eden. Some of the emigrants had the idea that there would be savage "Indians," while others had impressions of Canadians based on a little Dutch song: "There is that cousin from Canada, right in the heart of America, two meters high, three meters wide, no hair on his head, an empty cup, and a long thick beard. . . ." A short, stout man: that was a Canadian. That was the idea anyway, although the Canadian soldiers we had met certainly did not fit that description.

The dream became more of a possibility when one of our neighbours decided to emigrate to Canada to become farmers in Alberta. Because they didn't have the funds to move, they applied for a government subsidy, and when they received it they were enormously excited. With this example before us, we began to consider emigration seriously. We had some money through the business and could pay for the trip ourselves. If we had to start over, Canada, this peaceful country, seemed the right choice. If we did not succeed, then it would be our own fault and we would be the only ones to blame. We wouldn't be the scapegoats for other people's problems. We decided to apply.

The application required a great deal of information from us. All the members of our family had to be declared healthy, and it had to be shown that they were in good standing with the law. As a matter of fact, the authorities even went as far back as our parents, examining our whole family for character and honesty. Furthermore, we had to be sponsored by someone in Canada. I had an acquaintance in Holland who had a friend in Grenville, Quebec, who had been employed as a butcher in a small company called Arnold Farms, which specialized in horsemeat. Because he had decided to leave to start his own business, a replacement was needed. When the firm learned that Ernst knew the butcher's trade and even knew quite a bit about horses, they agreed to sponsor us. Once we were approved we put things together quite quickly.

To travel to Canada by boat with five children cost, if I remember correctly, about 3,000 guilders, which covered our tickets and a big wooden crate of luggage. This crate was brimful with linens and blankets, dishes, cutlery, pots and pans, clothes, and other odds and ends. Of course we also took with us the few little mementoes that were meaningful to us. Having heard that winters would be cold, I knitted a number of sweaters, cardigans and wool underwear. We sold all our furniture to cover the cost of the trip and gave the warehouse over to somebody else. After our trip was paid for, we had the equivalent of forty dollars for our new start in Canada.

The days of preparation flew by and, before we knew it, it was time to embark on the ship. The date was October 3, 1951. This day — when Ernst, I, and our five girls boarded the ocean liner, the *Volendam* — was one of the happiest and at the same time, one of the saddest days of my life. The *Volendam* would sail from Rotterdam straight to Quebec City. On the way we would pass England and a couple of islands, but after this, for eleven days we would not see anything on the wild Atlantic Ocean other than dark water and grey sky.

Once on board, we hung over the railing of the *Volendam*, waving at my family down below, laughing because we were happy to begin our new lives and crying over leaving my family on the quay. They were the only family we had left after the terrible war and the Holocaust. My two sisters and family waved back at us, smiling and crying and calling out messages. But it was hard to hear over all the other people shouting to their loved ones. We promised to visit each other. And then . . . the ropes to the quay were removed, the ramps pulled in, and suddenly the water between us became wider and wider. We threw kisses and made gestures of "I love you," while the people on the wharf grew smaller and smaller, and then, nothing. Having left behind our loved ones, our language and our country for a new and different way of life, we turned around to face our new country and destiny. We were entering another time of uncertainty in our life with no assurances that we would succeed in Canada. The only thing we were sure of was that Ernst had a job, and because of this we would have a roof over our heads.

The break from Holland was difficult, and for Elly it was especially traumatic. She was the oldest and had many good school friends. She loved her Aunt Jo greatly because she had been like a mother to her for the first years of her life. Jo's two oldest boys were like her brothers. For Johanna, our second child born during the war and eight years old by now, leaving Holland was also challenging. She had many good friends; she was always popular. Betty, our third daughter, found it less upsetting. She was six years old, and in the same year that we emigrated, her best friend and family left for Fort Saskatchewan, a little town close to Edmonton. The promise that one day she would see her friend again made her happy. However, as we were travelling to Grenville, Quebec, located close to the St. Lawrence River, we suspected that the reunion with her friend might never happen, and indeed it didn't. The youngest two did not comprehend much about the trip. They were not tall enough to look over the railing of the ship even when standing on their tiptoes. After we had disembarked in Quebec City, little Tikky asked me: "Mama, when do we go on the ship again?" On the ship they had felt fine; they had met so many new friends that any sadness was soon gone. Our being with them was all the assurance they needed.

I must tell you about the *Volendam*, the ship that would be our home for the next couple of weeks. The vessel was constructed so that the wealthy Dutch could visit the colonies in the East Indies.

All the high government positions in the colonies were filled by educated Dutch people who travelled once or twice a year back and forth to Holland, often with their whole families, nannies and servants. When the war started, and travel became too dangerous, this boat was converted to a troop transport. I think that the Germans even used it for awhile. Once the war was over, the boat was used as an emigrant ship. It had good services and because this trip from Holland to Canada would be its last one for 1951, there were an enormous number of people on board. In Canada, especially in the eastern provinces, ice was already forming on the rivers and canals. Soon the St. Lawrence River would be covered with an icy blanket and boats would not be able to reach Quebec before spring breakup. That was why we had to go now if we wanted to arrive this year. And we did. The employer wanted Ernst as soon as possible. In fact, it was one of the last voyages that this vessel would ever take. This boat had covered many miles on many oceans, likely starting early in the twentieth century, and it had begun to fall apart. We were not in danger, but after this trip it would be used only once more before being demolished.

Even though it was old and run-down, we could still see the splendour of this vessel. The large dining room where we ate our meals had once been used as the ballroom. Beautiful crystal chandeliers hung from the ceiling, and what was once a bar was decorated with brass or copper trimmings, while the barstools were covered with real leather, showing the rich past of the boat. No longer used to serve drinks, the bar was used as a station for the food, from where the waiters (and every table had a waiter) would bring meals to the tables. Since continual storms caused the boat to rock, we could not have carried the food ourselves. There were a large number of children on board, and at meal times they were strapped safely in their seats. I can tell you that between the soup and the main meal, several guests had to hurry to the ship's deck to hang over the railing to empty their stomachs. The fish must have appreciated it. Ernst did not have too much trouble, but I spent much of my time hanging over the railing, looking into the black water and breathing deeply, trying not to throw up.

Because there were so many emigrants on board, all our sleeping facilities were crowded. Men and women slept separately. Since the regulations were that men had their sons in their care and the women had their daughters, I had all the girls in my room. Had it been only me and the five girls, it would not have been too bad. However, in my room were three more women with their girls. Our sleep was regularly disturbed by someone crying or having to go to the bathroom. The bathroom was also a problem, for there were not enough stalls and you had to wait for each other. We had twenty women and girls and only one wash basin. You could not take a bath anyway; the water was sea water and the soap would not lather. In hindsight I suspect that our room was one of the better ones. It was located in the middle of the boat, so we did not feel as much swaying as Ernst did, sleeping with the men on a lower deck and closer to the front. At night when he went down to his bed it was nearly impossible to climb down, so the men just took a jump from the top of the stairs to the place where they slept. When the ocean was particularly turbulent, Ernst and some other men would creep upstairs and sleep the rest of the night in the little narrow hallway leading to the women's quarters.

During our voyage, I had time to think and I must admit that doubts began creeping in about our decision to leave Holland. We were always tired because the many storms on the Atlantic made it difficult to sleep. Despite the thoughtfulness of the ship's company, who tried to make everyone feel safe, the seas were rough and the swaying made us seasick. There was also much rain, buckets and buckets, which prevented us from going on deck. But as I think back, even in those times of bleakness and moments of doubt, I felt as though we were a big family who were, as the saying goes, "all in the same boat." We all had our personal reasons for burning our bridges behind us, although we did not talk too much about it. We made jokes, socialized and managed a few walks on deck when the weather wasn't stormy.

Once we were halfway across, our worries began to fall away. Somehow in this God-forsaken space on the dark, frightening Atlantic, a calm came over me. It was as if I could see back into my life and also far into the future. I knew then that we were right in our decision to go to Canada. The only thing that mattered now was that we were all on course to a new country — a country with open space, where there was a good chance that hard work and faith would earn each of us a living.

It was a pleasant thought to know that our children would be able to get ahead and could grow up free without all the red tape that the Dutch government imposed on its citizens. As I have mentioned, all our possibilities were restricted in Holland. If you wanted to start a business you first had to go to a special college to study. You had to know everything about the article you wanted to sell — where the material was found and how it was produced. You also needed a bookkeeper's diploma. On top of that, you had to show that you had enough money in the bank to support yourself for at least two years. Together, this would amount to 25,000 guilders. How many people had this kind of money after the war? If you had 250 guilders you were happy. Jobs were hard to find and even if you landed a job the wages were poor. I know that many of our friends would have loved to go with us to Canada if they had had the chance. Not because they did not love our country and our Queen. We all did, and before we made the decision we thought seriously about this important and irreversible move.

A large number of emigrants were farmers. On board we also had a fair number of factory workers skilled in their trades. In Holland they had been underpaid. At that time, Canada was asking for skilled workers and was offering high wages. Then there were the unskilled people. In Holland they did not have a chance to make a decent living. I believe that the governments of Canada and Holland chipped in to help pay for their voyage. Whereas Holland had no use for them, Canada wanted them for manual labour. It was hard for us to believe, but at this period manual labourers were paid well in Canada. As I say, it seemed that everybody had a chance in Canada. Women could also take a job if they wanted. In Holland this was not common. Jobs were scarce, so men had priority and the women stayed home and did the work a wife was "supposed" to do. We had the feeling that a wife did not really count.

For us, it was not only the better economy in Canada that mattered; we wanted to find a country where we, and in particular our children, would always live in freedom. It may be that the longing to go to a place where we felt wanted and where different nationalities and races were welcomed has been a continual hope and desire for the Jewish people. If you remember the stories in the Torah that refer to the suppression of the Jewish tribes, there was always the fear of being invaded by the surrounding enemies. Look at the story of Moses, who fled with all the Jewish slaves from Egypt. After living there for four hundred years as if it were their own land, they were still not welcome. I had an intense desire for a place that would welcome us. A place where we could belong.

Finally our voyage came to an end, and in the far distance we saw a shore and miniature trees. Entering the St. Lawrence River we were greeted by seagulls. By the time we could see more land and some buildings, a pilot boat had arrived to guide us further into the river so we could safely reach Quebec City. Here we would leave the ship and continue our trip by train. It was dark when our ship finally anchored and the steady drumming sounds of the engine stopped. We slept a little better that night, and then at about seven o'clock, there was a knock at our door with a message that breakfast was to be served and that we should get ready for disembarkation. For the first time in two weeks, I ate breakfast with a quiet stomach.

Some of our new friends were headed far inland to British Columbia. We thought "Oh, those poor people." At that time in Europe, the province of British Columbia was regarded as under-developed and full of "Indians." I wish we had known then what we knew later because we would have gone with them at that time instead of waiting for many years to make the journey to the West Coast. Vancouver at this time was a mid-sized, thriving metropolis; good jobs were plenty and starting your own business was easy. Instead, we accompanied our friends to the waiting train for Vancouver so we could say our goodbyes. Then we entered a hall where coffee and sandwiches were served. The different tables with refreshments represented different churches or organizations. We looked and looked, but there was no synagogue present for us. We must have been the only ones on board who were Jewish. We glanced at each other and shrugged, randomly choosing one of the tables and taking with thanks the food that was offered.

After our early lunch, we tried to figure out what to do with ourselves and our five tired children. It was late morning, but our train did not leave the station until midnight. Where could we go for the rest of the day? I dressed the girls in the warm wool sweaters and underwear I had knitted because it was already pretty chilly out. We decided to go into Quebec City to find a place where we could stay for the day until midnight. We saw many signs which said "*A Louer*" and one that said "Come In." We thought this must be a safe place to stay and that someone there must speak English. I knew a little bit of English from school and was sure that "Come In" indicated a welcoming, friendly place. Ernst put his suitcases down and while we waited for him on the street, he climbed the stairs to the apartment. When the door finally opened, Ernst was shocked to find a nearly naked woman standing before him. He quickly ran down the stairs. Apparently the signs "*A Louer*" (which normally means "to rent") and "Come In" were invitations to the male employees of ships that arrived daily in the harbour. It was a sort of red light district.

Finally we met a polite man who could speak English and he referred us to the St. Paul's Hotel where we were able to rent a room with two double beds for the day. We all took baths (our first in two weeks) and slept for more than four hours. After we were rested, Ernst went out to the grocery store to buy enough food to get us through the night and the final leg of our journey. We could not believe how much less the cost of food was in Canada compared to Holland. For less than two dollars he bought a loaf of white bread, a quart of milk, butter, cheese and some fruit.

After we had eaten and made some sandwiches to take with us

on the train ride, the children fell asleep again. Ernst and I were anxious to see more of this old city. We had noticed when we were leaving the ship that there was what looked to be a castle high on a mountain. We wanted to see the castle up close so we scanned the streets from our hotel window to figure out how we could reach it.

As we left for our little excursion, the young couple in the next hotel room promised to look in on the children now and then. At that time people were more trusting of each other than nowadays. We took the narrow and winding streets up towards the castle. The castle, however, did not appear to come any closer. We became tired and looked for somewhere to rest. In the distance we could see a restaurant with an advertisement for "B.B. Chicken." We did not know what "B.B." stood for but Ernst turned to me and said, "Let's try it." In Holland barbecuing was unknown and we thought that it must be something new, something Canadian. On board the ship we had already tried many new foods such as corn on the cob, corn soup and cornflakes. We ordered some of this chicken, which was served with french fries and another dish we did not know. It tasted very good and we thoroughly enjoyed it. Already we were beginning to like our new country.

By the time we were finished it was growing dark and we knew that we would not be able to reach the top of the mountain. Besides, we were anxious to get back to our children. We got up to pay the cashier and discovered that some of our stewards from the ship were also in the restaurant and eating this "B.B." chicken. It must have been a good little restaurant. One of the stewards said to us, "Good for you, to go out and enjoy yourselves. In the coming years you might not eat out again. You will have no time for it." I will never forget it. We thought she was joking, and we looked at her in disbelief, but we soon found out that she was right. For the next two years we worked very hard to buy what we needed for our children, pay for schooling and secure a down payment on a small house. But at that time in the restaurant, we just smiled and walked out the door.

When we arrived back at the hotel, we found Elly already dressing the younger ones. Elly was only eleven years old but she helped out all the time. She had spread out the coats on the beds ready for them to wear on the train because it was cold at night. At eleven o'clock we arrived at the station. We found the train already there, puffing smoke and working up clouds of steam. We boarded the train, found a compartment, rid ourselves of our heavy suitcases and made ourselves comfortable. At midnight the train chugged out of the station. But strangely enough we felt the train moving backwards; later on it began going forwards. This happened several times. The trip from Quebec City to Montreal took seven hours.

En route we noticed a young soldier sitting in the next compartment, who had the same figure and robustness of the Canadian soldiers that we had seen in Holland. He noticed that Ernst and I were very tired, so he helped throughout the night by keeping the small ones entertained. He took them on his knees and told them fairytales. They surely did not understand him but they felt safe with this boy. In Montreal we thanked him and wished him all the best for the future. He had talked with tremendous energy and hope about going out to fight and had explained how he felt he could really contribute to winning the war. Although he talked about Korea, I don't know if I understood which war he was referring to. Deep down in my soul I felt pity for this young man, who still thought that war was a thing to be proud of and that giving your life was honourable. In my mind I saw the graveyard close to the city of Nijmegen in Holland called the *Grebbeberg*, where many Canadian soldiers are buried: young men who all must have desired recognition for helping countries to escape the clutches of the German Reich. I was thankful that the Canadians had given their lives to liberate us, but what kind of honour is it to be dead and buried?

That night on the train from Quebec City to Montreal is engraved in my mind, and I feel now that I should have told the young soldier not to go into the army. But his enthusiasm was too sincere and I could not disappoint him. He was just a kid. Throughout the years I have often thought of him. I hope that he survived, that he returned to his family in one piece, and that he had a bright future. I would have liked to follow up, but I did not even learn his name.

We were very tired when we reached the central station in Montreal. Again we had to wait for a few hours until we could travel further. During this time we sat on hardwood benches in the ticket area, watching men sweep the floor. It seemed as though we watched for hours and hours. I was beginning to become agitated and anxious from the stress of travelling and lack of sleep, but finally we boarded the train to Grenville. We were on our last stretch of the journey. The train ride was uneventful and we were relieved and glad when the conductor called "Grenville!" This was it, we had arrived! The children, who were tired from travelling for two days, had slept a little during this one-hour ride, but now they were wide awake. We were all so happy that the journey was finally over. Our new adventures in Canada were about to begin. ·

It is here that I will put down my pen. But I close with these thoughts. After all my years in Canada, where we really found a sense of peace and freedom in the midst of our difficulties, I have discovered that I cannot escape my memories. They travelled with me. And so did that strange awkward sensation of feeling as if I were lost, that with the loss of our families we lost some of our bearings, our sense of home, and even a part of ourselves. Somewhere a part of me remains in hiding, silent, wandering. I live thousands of miles from Holland and am separated in time from the war and all its heartache by some sixty years, but my dreams still plague me. I still question why we were spared and not my parents and nearly all of our family. We were surely no better than the ones who were so unlucky to be murdered. Was it fate? Luck? Providence? Without really knowing the answers, I remain grateful for my life in Canada, for my wonderful children, grandchildren and great grandchildren, and the many years that Ernst and I shared together. And finally, I still have hope that human behaviour can change for the better. That my story might help.

Afterword

ROXSANE TANNER

To see someone's life all wrapped up in a book, so condensed yet so complete, can be unnerving. But it is even more disturbing when the person is your mother, and your mother is a Holocaust survivor. Between the two of them, Mama and Papa lost over one hundred people, including their own parents, almost all their siblings and many close friends. The Holocaust was an incredibly horrific, heinous crime that snuffed out the lives of innocent people because they were considered racially inferior. Mama and Papa were forced to leave their comfortable lives behind and survive for years with the fear of being discovered and killed. How do you live with that? How do you assimilate that knowledge, that reality, and make it through life unmarred? — knowing that you survived when so many didn't.

The story of Mama and Papa's lives during the war was never

discussed when we were young. They may have wanted to spare us the horrors of the war, or possibly the telling of the stories made the memories too difficult to bear. Being in a new country, they were determined to make a new life and leave the old behind. We knew that we didn't have grandparents and that they and some of our aunts and uncles were killed during the war. From history classes we learned about concentration camps and about how the Nazis killed the Jews. But apart from that, our parents' past remained largely a mystery to us.

During the war, Mama and Papa had to adjust very quickly to new situations that were totally out of their control. Their lives were in danger and they had to be continually aware of their surroundings and any signs of impending danger. After experiencing the terrors of the Holocaust, Mama and Papa were afraid for us, and when we arrived in Canada, they kept us close, and largely hid our Jewish identities from our friends and neighbours. We lived in mainly Christian communities and tried to blend in, all of which made us wonder in our early years if we should be ashamed of our religion.

The problems that Mama and Papa endured they endured in silence. Having lost everything in Holland, they had to start over again with five children in tow. In Canada they had an additional three children, making us a brood of eight. Mama and Papa were entrepreneurs and they worked very hard to provide for and support their family. We moved many times during our lives here in Canada as they pursued opportunities and planted new roots — only to have them torn up again in a very short time. We children had no say in the decision making. One day we would simply move, leaving schools and friends behind. After their experience in the Holocaust, Mama and Papa were determined to take control and make the best possible life for us.

It was very early in our upbringing when we realized that our home life as Jews, and especially as Jews who had survived the Holocaust, was different from that of other families. For one thing, the food was different. On our breakfast table there was always a

large assortment of cheeses, breads, matzos, Dutch rusks, choco-
late hail and boiled eggs. Who else has so much food for breakfast? Having lived through extreme austerity, Mama wanted to
ensure that her family was well fed. We were fed as royally as the
household budget would permit. At one point the family lived on
a street behind a vegetable market. Mama would go out to their
discard box, usually in the alley behind the store, and pick out
apples, pears or anything that could be salvaged. Just because it
was not marketable, didn't make it uneatable. Nothing should be
wasted in Mama's opinion. More often than not, dinner would
consist of a rich Dutch dish called Stumpot, which consisted of
potatoes mixed with sauerkraut or carrots and onions, covered
with gravy and topped with a huge chunk of meat. As well, great
bowls of soup with those lovely circles of fat floating on the surface were always served — and we would be in serious trouble if
we did not finish eating what was stacked on the plate!

Remembering the time they were in hiding when there was
never sufficient clothing, Mama never stopped knitting wool
sweaters for us (sweaters that scratched the living daylights out
of us). She also made comforters by quilting old army blankets together, obsessively stockpiling blankets and towels. And remembering how they had been separated from their two daughters when
they were in hiding, Mama and Papa could not imagine leaving us
alone with a babysitter. Always the family had to be together.

Mama and Papa were never allowed much time to grieve for
their losses. One of Mama's favourite stories was about the wool
coat that she had during the war. The coat was worn daily and as
it wore out, it went through a series of transformations until all
that was left of the coat were potholders. Each change in the original coat still had a purpose, proof that everything has its useful-
ness. Once in Canada, our difficulties were met in the same way:
what was done was done. We were told — as the Canadian expression has it — "to suck it in" and move on. Mama's remarkable per-
sonality, especially her optimism, her courage and determination,
became even more apparent as time went on. For example, she

tells in her memoir of how despondent she was when she had to leave her precious violin behind in the hospital where she worked — having to leave in a rush when she learned the Nazi soldiers were coming to clear out the hospital. She was only twenty years old at the time. What the book does not tell you is that she picked up the violin once again when she was seventy years old. She began taking lessons again and soon began playing beautifully.

Throughout her time in Canada, Mama was continually philosophizing about life, and this led her to write down her thoughts in poetry. She set down things the way she saw them. Her honesty was sometimes sharp, and she made her opinions well known. She handled adversity as a challenge. Mama always felt that she had a bigger purpose for living. She wondered why her life had been spared when so many were killed. She continually searched for that purpose in all aspects of her life. Even though there were many people who stole from her and were untrustworthy during the war, Mama emphasized the many wonderful people who risked their own lives to help them. She believed that the people who purposely do you harm would be taken care of by a higher power. I find it amazing that after all she suffered she still had such a positive attitude towards mankind.

The raising of her eight children was one of the most important things for Mama always. Mama sacrificed many luxuries in her life to provide for her family. She herself lived on a fixed budget, especially after Papa's death, but her generosity towards those in need was overwhelming. She reached out a helping hand to any needy person, family or friend.

As Mama grew older and her health began failing her, she felt a growing need to open the locked doors of her past and confront the horrors of her painful experiences during the war. She would go to universities to tell the students of her experiences during the Holocaust, to explain the life-and-death situations she encountered in hiding. She was concerned that she act as a witness to the Holocaust. Finally she decided to write down her story so as to purge any feelings of anger, hatred and guilt. By telling her story, she felt that could finally justify her existence. Papa had died at the age of seventy-two, unable to tell his story, and Mama didn't want that to happen to her. Mama was not a professional writer and it was a great effort for her to put down her story in words that would be her own and yet convey to others her experience of the Holocaust. Having now before me for the first time the full account of her life, I find myself astonished at what she lived through and what she has achieved.

Many things that my sisters and brother experience today are deeply imbedded in my mother's past, and as we read her memoir, we find thoughts and feelings rushing to the surface — things that only now are we able to understand. This is Mama's book, her memoir, but it is also a gift to us, her way of telling us what she could not speak. And now it is a gift to the world, a gift that teaches us how courage and love can transcend hatred.

Thank you, Mama.

Roxsane Tanner
for my sisters and brother

Index